YOUNG WRITERS

# Spellbound

## *LOTHIAN*

Poetry Now
YOUNG WRITERS

Edited By Simon Harwin

First published in Great Britain in 1998 by
*POETRY NOW YOUNG WRITERS*
1-2 Wainman Road, Woodston,
Peterborough, PE2 7BU
Telephone (01733) 230748



HB ISBN 0 75430 002 1
SB ISBN 0 75430 003 X

# *FOREWORD*

In this, our 5th competition year, we are proud to present *Spellbound Lothian.* This anthology represents the very best endeavours of the children from this region.

The standard of entries was high, which made the task of editing a difficult one, but nonetheless enjoyable. The variety of subject matter, creativity and imagination never ceases to amaze and is indeed an inspiration to us all.

This year's competition attracted the highest entry ever - over 46,000 from all over the UK, and for the first time included entries from English speaking children living abroad.

Congratulations to all the writers published in *Spellbound Lothian.* We hope you enjoy reading the poems and that your success will inspire you to continue writing in the future.

# *CONTENTS*

# *THE POEMS*

## The Sorcerer

Inside the sorcerer
The magic unwinds,
Magic so powerful,
The magic of all kinds.
The magic explodes
With an earth shuddering boom
And it turns chairs into tables
As it races around the room.

The books jump onto the table
And dance about with glee,
At last they are able to move,
The magic has set them free.
Pieces of paper fly about
Like a flock of frantic birds,
Then suddenly everything stops
As they hear the magic words.

The tables turn back into chairs,
The books jump into their case
The pieces of paper float down
And go back to their own place.
Now the room is quiet
It's as tranquil as the sky,
For the sorcerer is the ruler
And no one would dare defy.

***Emma-Jane Welsh (15)***

## VAMPIRE LOVE

Creatures of the night, so beautiful,
So scary.
Their eyes can steal your spirit,
For a dance in the demon moonlight, so wonderful,
Be wary,
Their beauty can steal your soul,
For a walk on the other side, so nice,
So risky.
Their bodies can steal your heart,
For a new beat of its drum, so lovely,
So in love.
Their mouths can steal your blood,
For an eternity of love, of torture,
Forever.

***Claire Louise Burgoyne (15)***

## ENGLISH

We all sat in the English classroom,
As she picked up a book and said,
'Listen now children a poem to hear,'
We all groaned as we shook our heads.
She looked at the poem and read it aloud,
With confidence, expression and meaning,
Not a word of sense did it make to us,
She noticed and continued her reading.
The second time, though, she explained it to us,
A piece of brown paper being crushed,
A daily event turned into a poem,
We chatted but immediately hushed.
'Can you write about anything?' she asked Stephen,
'Does it have to be special?' she asked me,
Then the bell rang and we were all happy,
As our faces were beaming with glee.
*'Homework,'* she shouted quite loudly,
As she outstretched her arms to the sky,
'Write a poem about the whole period
And *don't* bother to ask me why!'
So you see poetry can be about anything,
A field or a hot summer's day,
Life is a whole book of poems,
And that's basically what I wanted to say.

***Laura O'Donnell (13)***
***Bo'ness Academy***

## GHOSTLY GRANNY!

I've been inside Granny Smith's cottage,
It's haunted to say the least,
For every time you go inside it,
Out comes the Granny Smith beast!
She asks about school and offers you tea
At first she is nice,
(As you may see)
But then she goes cruel, then she goes mean,
Dr Jekyl fits the scene!
Blood red eyes, whitish hair,
Face of a werewolf,
(To be fair!)
But then she changes back
Everything's fine,
So I quickly run from Frankenstein!

***Laura Workman (11)***
***Boroughmuir High School***

## IT'S NOT MY FAULT

I wonder what they're doing,
That thing's pushing another thing.
It makes a horrible noise,
The other thing's watching a square box.
It makes a noise too,
What did I just say?
Oh well,
It's not my fault.

I'm a goldfish!

***Iain Welsh (12)***
***Boroughmuir High School***

## INFATUATION VS LOVE

A story of unrequited love
The love being mine for you
But not of you for I

Somehow in awe of you,
Your mind and your beauty
These spiritual admirations almost indescribable

Many and long
Are the days gazing at you
And the nights dreaming of you

Hoping, wishing you'd feel it too
But maybe you do
I'll never know, probably

Please let me in
And allow me to fulfil my driving ambition
To discover you, truly.

***Kirsty Gallacher (15)***
***Boroughmuir High School***

## THE BABY AND THE VAMPIRE

Her life so new will soon be mine,
I'll drink her blood as mortals do wine.

Her little pink cheeks are flowing with light,
Her little blonde locks like no child of the night.

Her blood flows through me like a bubbling stream,
It lulls me into a beautiful dream.

***Kirsty Orme (13)***
***Boroughmuir High School***

## The Rainbow

The lush colours shine through my eyes,
As ultra-violet rays beam down from the skies,
Raindrops fall from it like running paint,
You can hear laughter ringing in your ears which is very quiet and faint.
The leprechauns leap and slide down the beams,
Glittering,
Sparkling,
Twinkling,
As shining as the sun,
As bright as a star,
As brilliant as the moon,
Lying deep in the sky afar,
Where did it come from?
Why is it here?
It looks like a paint bomb,
In our hemisphere.
It is happiness and not a foe,
It's our dear friend little rainbow.

***Ellie Jones (12)***
***Boroughmuir High School***

## Winter

W is for the *windy* nights that chill your little bones
I is for freezing *infants*, all you year from them are moans!
N is the *nature* trying to keep warm
T is for the *tremendous*, scary storm
E is the *enchantment,* for Christmas time is near,
R is for *Rudolph,* the red nosed reindeer.

***Genevieve Ryan (12)***
***Boroughmuir High School***

## Bullying

I don't know why
it seems to be,
but everybody picks on me.
They call me names
I want to cry
and really I just don't know why.

I'd sit in class,
all on my own
(I'm sorry if this sounds a moan)
it would be nice,
if there could be,
a friend - who sits right here with me.

The problem can be overcome,
the answer is to tell someone,
that you can trust, to help you through
and squeeze the bullies out of you.

***Louise Bingham (12)***
***Boroughmuir High School***

## Why?

Why say you'll call when you won't
Why say you love me when you don't?
Why say you'll meet me when you're never around
Why does everything you say make me fall to the ground?
Why when you call does my life have to halt
Why oh why is it really my fault?
Why stay together when we know it won't last
Why don't we let *us* fall into the past,
Why?

***Lesley Cowie (15)***
***Boroughmuir High School***

## Learning Golf

Went to the Braids for a swing or two,
Couldn't get the action properly through.
Couldn't hit that very small ball,
But when watching the pros it didn't look hard at all.

Swing again and watch the turf fly,
It wasn't the ball but I still won't cry,
Instead give it a couple more tries.

Connect with the ball,
It only goes a yard or two,
This could possibly not be true.
Could hardly believe,
I'd hit the ball,
Maybe football isn't my only game at all.

One day
I'll become a pro,
Because I've determination
That I know.

***Mark Antoni (12)***
***Boroughmuir High School***

## Stars

S hining across the midnight sky,
T he twinkling and sparkling catches my eye,
A round the sky the stars appear,
R eaching out for the stars, I fear,
S tars are far away, not near.

***Lindsay Sharp (12)***
***Boroughmuir High School***

## WINTER

Winter is when the snow falls
Which makes a white sheet over
Distant cities.
The children walk to school
Jumping through each other's footprints.
Snowmen look at you with their beady
Eyes like you are famous.
A little boy tries to break the ice off a
Pond in his local park.
Radiators are turned to full
To keep people warm.
Decorations are put out to brighten
Up the Christmas tree,
So that's why I enjoy *winter.*

***Mark Parry (11)***
***Boroughmuir High School***

## THE SPRING LAMBS

As jumpy as spring we play around
As small as a rock we appear
We suckle from our mothers like
newborn babies
When summer comes, we play around
Like little rabbits.
We like the winter when the
snow is lying on the ground.
Our tails spin like Catherine wheels.
We are as soft as the fluffy
white clouds.

***Katie Mary Dawson (12)***
***Boroughmuir High School***

## DREAM PONY

I see a pony behind the trees
I whistle softly through the breeze
She looks up,
She canters down.
Her angelic face I stroke,
She takes an apple from my hand
Her velveteen lips, so soft and sweet,
Gently cup my hands while she eats.

Her halter's on and I lead her about
I put on her saddle and we go out
We gallop through a field encrusted with snow,
Now I know why I love her so.
We approach a ditch and she takes off -
Will she jump it or will she not?
But she sails over it with the greatest of ease
Again I feel the breeze and I realise what a lovely
Day-dream that has been.

***Lucy Dobson (13)***
***Boroughmuir High School***

## HEARTS FC

H ibs are their rivals,
E urope is their destiny
A lways scoring goals
R elegation is what they despise
T ynecastle is their stadium
S coring goals is their tradition.

***Duncan Manson (12)***
***Boroughmuir High School***

## CHOCOLATE

I love chocolate
It's so delicious
My mum always tells me
*'It's not nutritious'*

Dark chocolate's the best
Better than all the rest
Milk chocolate is okay
Even though it makes your teeth decay

But least of all white chocolate
I will never keep in my pocket.

***Emily Munro (11)***
***Boroughmuir High School***

## ROSES

Roses are love in the sky,
Roses are so lovely it makes me want to cry,
Roses are my mum's cheeks when she says goodbye,
That's what roses are,
Roses make me happy,
Roses make me sad,
Roses make me cheery,
Roses are a part of me that makes me feel so weary.
Roses are the sun in me
Roses make me happy as can be,
That's why roses are roses
I love roses.

***Callum MacMichael (13)***
***Boroughmuir High School***

## Sadist Insect

Unlike bees, who are careful with their stings,
Those annoying little wasps are sadistic little things.

As he's zooming down with the stinger sharpened,
You can see his face light up as his victim starts to scarper.

The victim thinks he's lost his foe but unfortunately for him,
His attacker is still zooming down with an evil little grin.

As the target lashes out the wasp ducks and dives,
He's done this many times before: it's on spreading pain he thrives.

As the stinger gets stuck in the boy lets out a yell,
'You stupid little parasite! You can go to hell!'

The wasp receives a glancing blow and smashes into a wall,
As he slides off the bricks his *flying* turns to *fall*.

The wasp falters, coughs and splutters as his vision starts to fade,
As the foot comes closer he knows that for his sins he's paid.

***Andy Stevenson (13)***
***Boroughmuir High School***

## Begging

Sitting on a doorstep
A hat in front of me
A few coins lying in it
My hands and legs are numb with cold
People passing pretend they can't see
But they can
Children come and drop in coins
'Sometimes'
All I want to do is die!

***Sasha Watson (11)***
***Boroughmuir High School***

## Mermaid

Your tumbling curls about your face,
So pale and white
So fierce but mild.

Your face prettier than any mortal I've seen
Your eyes like thunderstorms.

As I look you see me not but I see
Waves crashing in your heart, in mine.

Then as you turn you see me
And then have gone to the
Depths of the sea.

For you have gone
Have gone away
Never to return to my lonely bay.

***Verity Cumming (12)***
***Boroughmuir High School***

## Running

There once was a boy who ran a mile
But he couldn't for quite a while
All because he fell on a stone brick
Which made him very sick
So he decided to play a trick on his friends
As they made fun of him at school
Just because they thought it was cool
So he made up a plan
Which made them run
And that made him run again.

***Brooke Miller (12)***
***Boroughmuir High School***

## Autumn Time

Autumn,
The leaves falling off the trees,
Are stood on
Crunch, crunch, crunch, crunch.

Golden leaves,
Fluttering to the ground,
Are stood on
Crunch, crunch, crunch, crunch.

Bronze leaves,
Falling to the ground,
Are stood on
Crunch, crunch, crunch, crunch.

Then winter comes,
Crunch, crunch, crunch, crunch,
In the snow!

***Elizabeth Dunn (11)***
***Boroughmuir High School***

## Tipp-Ex

Tipp-Ex, Tipp-Ex,
On my chair,
Tipp-Ex, Tipp-Ex,
Everywhere,
Tipp-Ex, Tipp-Ex,
Makes a mess
Oh look I've got it on my dress
Oh my gosh it's made a stain
I'll never use Tipp-Ex
*Again.*

***Stephanie Gilmour (11)***
***Boroughmuir High School***

## Cat And Mouse

With malicious intentions,
She stalks,
The corridors,
Until she finds,
The mice,
Of her desire,
Like a cat,
She plays with us,
Until she's bored,
With her prey,
And with,
A sarcastic remark,
Meant to hurt,
She leaves.

***Emma Nock (14)***
***Boroughmuir High School***

## Exam Stress

Sitting,
A feeling of dread
Waiting,
Hands shaking
Revising
Minds exploding with facts
Thinking,
Of calm thoughts and tranquillity
Remembering,
Past knowledge and feeling
Stressed,
At this moment in time.

***Kirin Jeffery (15)***
***Boroughmuir High School***

## The Dark Mornings

I'm dragged from a blissful, warm place,
to a cold, dark room at 6.30am.
I feel dead.
I walk in a dark, thirsty daze to a destination,
where I am greeted with a glass of orange juice and
a bowl of Cheerios (yeah right).
I feel dead.
I stagger out into the darkness,
only to be blinded by the intensity of the security light.
I feel dead.
I cycle along the road, cold and miserable,
and nearly get killed by a car.
I could be dead.
I pedal around, delivering folk's papers,
lucky people, still in bed.
I feel dead.
I struggle up my street which feels like a 1 in 2 gradient,
and collapse into the house, which reminds me of a furnace.
I feel dead.
I bravely face the half hour walk to school,
and as I step into the building I remember I've got English.
I wish I was dead.

***David Crawley (14)***
***Boroughmuir High School***

## My Limerick

There once was a boy called Norman
Who went to the zoo with Herman
They captured a baboon
And made it eat oatmeal with a spoon
And now it lives beside a chubby racoon.

***Craig Ward (12)***
***Boroughmuir High School***

## Newspapers

It doesn't really look all that important:
Just thousands of words,
Just tens of pages.
Still it's the story of the world
At least, for today
To let people know what's happening
Is a wonderful gift
And through this wonder of news
This gift is shared with us all

It doesn't really look all that important:
Just thousands of words,
Just tens of pages.
Still it's the story of the world
In one place it's written
In thousands of places it happens
Newspapers,
Written for millions of people
Written about millions of people.

***Neil Cardwell (14)***
***Boroughmuir High School***

## A Christmas Surprise

I'm up in the morning and it's half-past five
I'm going down the stairs to get my Christmas surprise
There it is it's red with a bow but
What's inside? I'm dying to know
With a bump and a thump it's moving all alone
Oh wow it's a puppy of my very own.

***Leyla Cameron***
***Boroughmuir High School***

## THE SEASONS

Spring, then summer,
Autumn, winter
Slowly coming
Slowly leaving.

Each season has its turn,
It's like a large cartwheel
Slowly but surely turning
Around and around and around.

First in line is springtime,
A lovely time of year
A new beginning for everyone
relaxed and calm and happy.

Next in line is summer,
My favourite time of year
The fun filled holiday season
That everyone just loves.

The third in line is autumn,
When the leaves fall from the trees
Coating the ground in a layer of colour
Leaves crisp and crackly dry and brown.

The final season's winter,
With snow that coats the ground
For miles white snow gleams in the sun
That pokes through the white and fluffy clouds.

The year is old and finished now,
And fields lay bare and empty
But there's no need to worry
As spring is nearly here.

***Jamie Crawford (12)***
***Boroughmuir High School***

## Virus

I am in front of my computer,
Doing my homework.
I have almost finished,
Then the screen goes blank.
It then goes speckly and I see myself,
On the screen I am in front of a computer,
Doing my homework.
Then I watch as the computer on the screen explodes,
On my monitor the words *Game Over* appear in bright red.
Then a photo of my family appears on the screen,
It shows my mum, my dad and my brother,
They are leaning over a small grave in our garden.
I am not in the picture,
I have been killed.

***Joe Mathieson (11)***
***Boroughmuir High School***

## An Ode To Scratch

The gerbil took the agility
of the squirrel;
The high jump of the kangaroo;
The nip of the chipmunk;
The shiny coat from the sly, sly cat,
Then it stole the tail of the monkey,
And
the
gerbil
was
born.

***Eddie Ross (11)***
***Boroughmuir High School***

## STALLION

His eyes as black
As the colour of night
His nostrils flaring
Like a flaming coal
His movement so graceful
At every sight

He twists and turns
Like a whirlwind whirls
His coat so black
That he melts into the dark

You can see the sparks as his
Shoes strike stones
Along the way of the bending trees

As dawn breaks
You can see him now
His tail swishing at a happy sight
His stallion coat gleaming in the light
As he gallops off over his pasture
Back to his herd.

***Louise Cumming (12)***
***Boroughmuir High School***

## FIELD MOUSE

Cute and small,
He rustles his way through the field,
His little nose twitching, his heart pounding,
As he looks for something nice to eat.

He clambers up the corn,
Then suddenly, out of the sky,
Comes an eagle.
With one almighty swoop he catches the mouse
Then he flies off to eat his prey.

***Elise Cunningham (12)***
***Boroughmuir High School***

## JUST ANOTHER DAY

It's that big hill again
For the third time today
I can hear her crying
Like every other day

I see an old lady
Who gives me a look
I know I'm not perfect
But there's no need to look

I'm getting to the top
To my tiny little flat
I live on the thirteenth floor
With my baby and the cat

The house will be empty
With nobody home
I'll listen to the radio
To drown out her moan

I'll look forward to tomorrow
It's a brand new day
But for me and my baby
It's just another day.

***Kim Fraser (15)***
***Boroughmuir High School***

## Relationships

Relationships, what are they?
They never last as long as hoped,
The expectation is high and friends are more
Excited than the two involved.

Relationships are usually great to start with.
They go out, have fun, enjoying each other's company,
They have passion, at least for a while.

Relationships! Why do people spread rumours
which spoil it all.
They all say he said this and she said that
while none of it is true.
This is what really tests relationships.
Will they discard this as a lot of fun?
Do they hell!

Relationships, who needs them?
Because all they mean is trouble.

***Jeremy Klayman (13)***
***Boroughmuir High School***

## Gran

The shock through my body
While I was told
I was only ten years old
The days of crying
The days of lying
I wondered: why oh why
Did my gran have to die?

***Kirsten McIlwraith (12)***
***Boroughmuir High School***

## YOU MAKE ME FEEL

You make me feel like a rose
You make me feel like a star
You make me feel as if I am an angel
You make me feel free
You make me feel like a million pounds
You make me feel like a queen
You make me feel good inside
You make me feel as if my heart has stopped beating
You make me feel sick
You make me feel sad
You make me feel scared
You make me feel poor
You make me feel like I have been kicked to the
bottom of the sea
You make me feel like nothing, as if I was not there
You make me feel terrible.

You make me feel.

***Charmaine Douglas (11)***
***Boroughmuir High School***

## DREAMS

People do not realise,
We lead alternate lives,
In alternate universes,
All inside our minds.
For when we sleep and dream at night,
We dream alternate worlds,
Patched together from memories,
Forgotten long ago.

***Iain Macleod (14)***
***Boroughmuir High School***

## The Christmas Tree

Cut down in her prime,
Not living all her time.
Little Christmas tree is cut,
Then she is taken to a hut.

Mr Field takes her in his car,
They travel very very far.
Soon they come to the gate,
By then it's getting quite late.

They get inside and see,
Children jumping up with glee.
The presents all ready, in piles,
A tired face sees her, smiles.

She dons her angel, baubles and light,
Something is drawing in, the night.
She sees her time will not be bad,
So there's no reason to be sad.

***Shona Newton (12)***
***Boroughmuir High School***

## My Bath Tub

My bath tub is white
My bath tub is bright
My bath tub keeps me warm
Through morning to night.
I go there stressed and I have
A long rest
Knowing I will come out my best.
There is no other place I would rather be,
Because my bath tub is my castle to me.

***Lee Calder (15)***
***Boroughmuir High School***

## THE BEACH

Walking along the sandy beach,
Watching the deep sea.
Seeing how far the waves will reach,
Hoping they won't reach me.

Admiring all the pretty shells,
Moving with the waves.
Smelling all the seaside smells,
As I explore the caves.

I watch the noisy seagulls soar,
In the waves the fishes play.
The crabs scuttle across the shore,
As the sandworms wriggle away.

On the beach I see shells and stones,
I step on them and hurt my feet.
The very strong wind loudly moans,
As myself and the water meet.

***Laura Murphy (14)***
***Boroughmuir High School***

## HAVE YOU EVER SEEN A . . .

Have you ever seen a shark
Man-eating, never sleeping, large toothed?

Have you ever seen a gerbil
Long tailed, fast running, grain eating?

Have you ever seen an alien
Green skinned, big headed, large eyed?

***Gary Reid (12)***
***Boroughmuir High School***

## The Journey Home

When the bell rings we are told to be quiet,
But instead there's a riot.
We all rush
To catch the bus
There is a tremendous crush

On the bus, it takes ages
And there are enormous rages
Eventually, I get to the stop
And I start to walk
Up the road to my house

I walk in the door
Throw my bag on the floor
Then I get a drink
And start to think
What will I do today?

***Graham Emerson (12)***
***Boroughmuir High School***

## Tipp-Ex

Tipp-Ex, it goes everywhere,
On her table and on her chair.
Never goes where she wants it to,
Against Tipp-Ex she will always lose.
Though it usefully covers her mistakes,
Until it turns to dried up flakes.
It should be used as liquid gold,
But she has been far too bold.
Listen to the teacher shout:
'Why can't you simply score it out?'

***Sarah Rankine (14)***
***Boroughmuir High School***

## Sweet Dreams

I love to lie there and sleep
but I dread that alarm bleep

It startles me out of my haze
and into bright new days

My dreams are lovely and beautiful
though never dull and dutiful

But nightmares are dark and scary
I wake and I am weary

On my bed my sheets are white
ready for another night

In my dreams I laugh and play
I wish I could forever stay

My bed is cosy and always gleaming
I lie down and start dreaming.

***Peter Walker (13)***
***Boroughmuir High School***

## Silently

Silently I tiptoe to the kitchen;
Silently I start to eat last night's chicken;
Silently my sister Raisa sneaks up on me;
Silently she sits on my knee;
Silently we start to talk;
Silently we start to walk;
Silently we go to sleep;
Silently I dream about the deep.

***Scheila Silveira (12)***
***Boroughmuir High School***

## Enemy Lock-On

The molecules of the air are split
By the firing of the hungry bullet,
It searches for its target,
And once near,
It ploughs in so hard,
That the blood and tissue may lead it,
Never to be discovered.
The pain overcomes the bad guy,
As he struggles to escape,
His eyes are now bloody,
And the evil stench of death,
Is now rampant.

In his last seconds he asks himself,
Why his number came up so soon.

However, for the killer, this is something
Which could make him a fortune,
But the murderer has killed
An innocent animal and that seems as
Evil as the

Billions who do nothing to stop them.

***Stephen Christie (14)***
***Boroughmuir High School***

## Dirty Old Tube Trains

Dirty old tube trains underground,
Dirty old tube trains under the town,
Stopping and starting all the way,
Carrying passengers for the whole day.

'Mind the gap!' the announcements say,
Then they tell you there's been a delay.
Charing Cross, Oxford Street, Camden Town.
They all whiz past when you're underground.

***Gordon Douglas Stevenson (12)***
***Boroughmuir High School***

## A Deserted House

In the hallway . . .
 Pictures hang with broken glass
 A phone lies on the floor
 Children's toys lie scattered about
And the sun shines through the door.

In the bedroom . . .
 A window with curtains blowing around
 The bed all torn and ripped
 Perfume bottles lying about
And a laugh echoing in the air.

In the study . . .
 Paper falling from the desk
 Files sticking out from the drawers
 Old trophies from years ago
And glass from the window broken on the floor.

In the playroom . . .
 A rocking horse moves in the wind
 Teddies and dolls a little brown mouse
 Clothes of the dolls lie around
And I smile as I leave the house.

***Rachael Docking (11)***
***Boroughmuir High School***

## NEW DAY

As the sun rose still higher to the sky,
Many soft sounds could be heard,
The birds' morning song,
The splish-splash of fish in the river,
The dawn chorus is up,
It's the start of a new day.

As the light increases,
The shadows fade away,
The sight of the rising sun,
Takes a passer's breath away:
It's the start of a new day.

As the brightness touches the flowers,
They open to praise the sun,
The smell of spring drifts in the air,
Sweet and new, scents diffuse the land:
It's the start of a brand new day.

***Chloë Capewell (13)***
***Boroughmuir High School***

## BULLIES

Bullies
Mean, cruel
Always hurting people
Never leave them alone
Always pestering, whispering horrible things
Nasty, not wanted, cruel
Hitting, punching, kicking
Go away
Go!

***Rachel Craik (12)***
***Boroughmuir High School***

## I Wish

I wish I could live in a faraway land
With the bright orange fish and the glittering sand.

I wish that I was a billionaire
So I could fly through the peaceful air.

I wish I had a big posh car
So I could drive away very far.

I wish I had a year's supply of
Cadbury's milky chocolate bars.

***Laura McKenzie (12)***
***Boroughmuir High School***

## The Fat Black Cat

There was a black cat,
He was a very fat cat at that,
And he lived on the eleventh floor,
In a big tall flat.

He liked to sit on the door mat,
And he sat and sat and sat.

Sometimes he miaowed,
And sometimes he woofed,
As you can see it was a very strange cat,
Who liked to sit on the bristly door mat.

***Lindsay Kemp (11)***
***Boroughmuir High School***

## The Beach

I see golden sand
I hear the waves crashing against the shore
I feel the heat of the sun on my skin
I smell the salty air
I taste my strawberry ice-cream.

***Sophie Cartmell (12)***
***Boroughmuir High School***

## Lies

Lies are terrible
Lies are white
Lies are secret protectors
Lies are rule benders
Lies are spread
Lies are bad feeling makers.

***Natalie Redmond (12)***
***Boroughmuir High School***

## Schools Are . . .

Schools are boring,
Schools are like deep, dark dungeons,
Schools are workplaces,
Schools are places of dread on a Monday morning,
Schools are great on a Friday half-day.

***Mark Pettie (12)***
***Boroughmuir High School***

## Have You Ever Seen?

Have you ever seen a aeroplane
Big white giant on a cloudy sky?

Have you ever seen a high speed train
Killing peace on a sunny day?

Have you ever seen a football crowd
Screaming, shouting at a game?

Have you ever seen a speeding car
Chasing, racing at a rally?

***Scott Simpson (12)***
***Boroughmuir High School***

## Jack

My friend Jack is very small,
It takes him four days to walk up the hall.

People have to watch out in case they squish him,
Or else he's dead, dead as a door-pin.

Why, why did he not scream
When someone crushed him like a bean?

But now the hall is in a bit of a guddle,
With his bits and bobs lying in a puddle.

***Peter Crayk (12)***
***Boroughmuir High School***

## CHRISTMAS

I hate Christmas
It's strange I know,
But that's the way I feel.

You may ask why,
How could anyone,
Hate Christmas?

All those months' preparation,
All that lively decoration,
And all those presents.

But my view is different,
Twisted in a way,
I see it through frosted glass.

I spend months on end,
Getting ready,
Shopping and thinking.

I climb a hill,
Slowly,
From October to December.

Then I reach the cliff top,
I fall, it's over,
It's December 26th.

***Ellie Maizels (13)***
***Boroughmuir High School***

## SUDDENLY

Suddenly the boy slips into the lake
Suddenly the man gets bitten by a snake
Suddenly a girl gets killed by a gun
Suddenly a woman turns into a nun.

Suddenly the dog gets a big fright
Suddenly the jumper is far too tight
Suddenly the cat slips on the rug
Suddenly the kid gets bitten by a bug.

***Rosie Armitage (11)***
***Boroughmuir High School***

## Dogs Are

Dogs are soft and cuddly
Dogs are slow until they run
Dogs are cuddly until they bite
Dogs are cute when they are pups
Dogs are hungry until they eat
Dogs are smelly when they are wet.

***Michelle Malone (11)***
***Boroughmuir High School***

## Maybe

Maybe the dead will come tomorrow
Maybe they'll scare us

Maybe the world will end tomorrow
Maybe the sun will turn cold

Maybe I'll die tomorrow
But, then again, maybe I won't.

***Larisa Butenko (15)***
***Boroughmuir High School***

## THE IGYWIGGYWAZLEPOP-TIDDLEWAZOO

The Igywiggywazlepop-Tiddlewazoo,
has no set habitat and lives in no zoo.
It has no set predators and no set prey,
but does enjoy half a pound of insects every day.

All who see it die insane,
unable to explain,
the brilliance of this remarkable creature,
or any one single feature.

It lurks in the mountains of Tibet,
and in the Highlands' constant wet.
Oh my my my . . . what a coo
The *Igywiggywazlepop-Tiddlewazoo.*

***Alex Martin (13)***
***Boroughmuir High School***

## MY TWO BEST FRIENDS

I have two best friends named Katie and Michelle
They hate each other like hell.
They used to be best friends
Now their friendship's come to an end.
I don't want to boast
But I like them both.
Michelle is nice
But is square as a dice.
Kate is an excellent friend as well
But I wish they would make up 'cause that would be
*Swell!*

***Isma Durrani (12)***
***Boroughmuir High School***

## Football Match

I wish that I could be there,
Where adult men go to swear.
They shout and bawl at the referee,
And point out what a plonker is he,
This slightly discourages me from
Becoming a football ref when I grow up.

After the match a fight will start here
Where people throw bricks and
Bottles of beer,
This is okay and could go on all day,
But then the police come along and
Take you away, then charge you with
Assault and damage of property

Football, what a wonderful game.

***Bruce Cameron (13)***
***Boroughmuir High School***

## Noses

Smelling machines
That work night and day
Smelling what's cooking
For today's tea

Working in the high street
Working in the back street
They're always working
*Noses.*

***Alasdair Scott (11)***
***Boroughmuir High School***

## Out Of School

End of the day,
Out of school,
Trying my hardest to keep my cool.
Wondering what will happen now . . .
As I walk through the school gates
I wonder how I can avoid the terror that
Waits for me.
I think I'm safe,
But what do I see:
A group of people, coming my way!
How do I keep my fate at bay?
I could run back to school and hide my face,
But I know they're certain to keep the pace;
I could lower my head and walk on by,
But I've already noticed the hate in their eyes,
So I might as well wait,
Wait and see,
What they have in store for me,
Will I be black and blue, covered in red?
I won't be surprised if I end up dead.
But what is this?
They're walking on by!
Have they forgotten the reason why
They want to get me?
Or maybe they don't,
Right now my heart is full of hope that
I won't see them again,
That they'll go away.
Or will they come back, another day?

***Susanna Klayman (14)***
***Boroughmuir High School***

## THE WALTZERS

It stars off slow and gets faster and faster,
You start to turn, and you go round and round,
Then you get thrown backwards, into the back of your seat.
The music is blasting in your ears, and the lights are shining
in your eyes.

You go round and round and up and down,
Then it gets slower,
And slower,
And even slower,
Then it stops.

***Rosie Hawley (12)***
***Boroughmuir High School***

## HALLOWE'EN

H allowe'en, Hallowe'en, I can hear the witches scream,
A pumpkin smashes a vampire to ashes,
L ove is fierce, and the Cyclops nears,
L anterns are burning, the clouds are turning,
O gres roar, in a hurry guisers close their doors,
W itches scream in the dead of night,
E erie songs and eerie lights,
E verybody screams and lots of frights,
N ow the real fun has begun, Hallowe'en oh Hallowe'en.

***Amy Neilson (12)***
***Boroughmuir High School***

## MUSIC BOX DOLL

Head that is poised
Arms that are lifted
Feet in position
Toes that are pointed
Gracefully curving
And lifting
And stretching
Eyes that are fixed
And concentrating hard
Inside the head
All thoughts but one, are barred
Everything beautiful
Lonely and sad
Pirouette to lift
Arms must be higher
Back must be straight
Be light on your toes
And yet behind all this beauty
Another girl grows
Desolate and fearful of stopping or going wrong
She must keep in time with the music box song
Then with a snap she is stopped as if dead
Another year overtakes her now
How long will this darkness all of her shroud
On her life goes full of wishes and dreams
Trying to be graceful beyond her means
And then one day when the music box stops
The beautiful ballet dancer
Herself, will drop.

***Gail MacLeod (14)***
***Boroughmuir High School***

## A Day In The Park

I wander through the park, with Minty my dog,
It's an autumn day, there's leaves on the ground.
I throw Minty's ball and it lands in the lake,
I whisper 'Go get it!' and she bounds away,
Leaps into the lake and hunts for the ball,
Disturbing all the ducks so they fly away.
She's found the ball and brings it to me,
Soaking wet and wagging her tail.
We wander home through the fallen leaves.

***Janet Shepherd (12)***
***Boroughmuir High School***

## Do The Dishes!

No because . . . The dog's at my throat
The bubbles won't float
The cat's on the brink
There's sharks in the sink
The sink's got a leak
My future looks bleak
My homework's not done
I'm going out for some fun
I burst the car tyre
Don't call me a liar, so . . .
Why don't *you* do the dishes?

***Greg Ewens (12)***
***Boroughmuir High School***

## All Through The Year

Spring
In the spring daffodils grow,
Lambs are born
And the weather gets warm.
The sun shines down on us
We are glad to see it again.
The weather is warmer.

Summer
The sun pours down on us now
And the summer holidays are here
Some of us go away on vacation
Others stay at home.

Autumn
In the autumn the leaves change colour
They turn red, brown, yellow and orange
And who knows what else.
This is when the weather gets colder.

Winter
In the winter the birds fly away
And the snow sometimes falls all day
It's freezing cold
So you have to wrap up tight
And make sure you have a snowball fight
Then *yes* at last it's come
It's Christmas
Then next thing you know
It's a brand new year
And you're back to school
Doing school work and homework.

The year
*Spring* is pretty full with flowers
*Summer* is hot full with fun
*Autumn* is beautiful full with lots of colours
*Winter* is cold with surprises and snow fights
*The whole year* is full of different wonderful things.

***Holly Thornthwaite (11)***
***Boroughmuir High School***

## HAMSTER

Looking out through the bars of my cage,
Doomed to live my life in this horrid, horrid maze.
As I gaze at the freedom you have,
I wonder how you'd feel.
Trapped like a rat in a trap,
As I run on my little wheel.
Day,
Night,
Night,
Day,
Always the same . . . same . . . same . . .

***Christopher Main (12)***
***Boroughmuir High School***

## LIFE

This can last as long as you want it,
And is more precious than diamonds and gold.
From dusk till dawn we try to enjoy it,
And day by day we want to improve it.
So, why do people want to abuse it,
By taking drugs and losing it?

***Gillian Reid (15)***
***Boroughmuir High School***

## The Cat

There was a fat cat,
Who had a plait,
He went to his mat
But on his way he tripped,
And went
*Kersplat!*

***Stephanie Williamson (12)***
***Boroughmuir High School***

## People

I'm slick, I'm slack, I'm Johnny Black
I'm short, I'm thin, I'm Jamie Pin
I'm tall, I'm fat, I'm Jeremy Platt
I'm scared, I'm sad, I'm Tony Glad
I'm cool, I'm radge, I'm Alex Bad
I'm funny, I'm smart, I'm Ross Dart.

***Steven Nicol (12)***
***Boroughmuir High School***

## Spring

Its petals are as red as blood
They feel as smooth as plastic
Bobbing up and down in a bunch
The smell of pollen attracts the bees

I hear a buzzing noise coming from inside
I look
A bee comes out and stings me.

***Ian Packwood (12)***
***Carmondean Primary School***

## Spring Poem

I hear . . . lots of bees buzzing and lambs calling,
I see . . . flowers growing and happiness everywhere,
I smell . . . the sweet scents from all the flowers,
I think . . . about the sun shining and tadpoles forming frogs,
I touch . . . beautiful swans and all the birds,
I wish . . . spring would stay forever and ever.

***Nicola Fleming (12)***
***Carmondean Primary School***

## On A Plane

On a plane,
Up so high,
A field of fluffy clouds,
Looking down,
My heart beginning to race,
Then
slowly
we
are
going
d
o
w
n
again,
Then we land,
And
Go to bed
In a nice, cosy house,
again!

***Alana Shaw (11)***
***Drummond Community High School***

## ISLAMABAD

This morning I watched the sun
rise upon me like a glowing pumpkin
the brightness giving the unknown night a name.
Cars raced by and skeletons were shouting
and screaming over the roof of the high tops.
Planes landing, luggage pushed around,
skeletons tripping each other
and making their way out of the darkness.
Clothes everywhere.
I see different colours, materials of all sorts
scattered on a stall like the one I saw in my dream.
I can hear shouting, screaming in the background.
But can't put the voices and faces together
as there are too many.
Still not quiet although night has come in.
I lie restless and hope for the noises to go away.

***Nehla Javid (15)***
***Drummond Community High School***

## PLANES

Planes are huge and some are tiny
Planes are lazy and pretty speedy
Some are charming and some are dreadful
There are lots of different kinds.
Some of them new and some of them old
Some hold lots of people some hold none
You have to pay a lot to get on it
But when you do you'll have a good flight
Maybe you'll even stay the week.

***Kevin MacGregor (12)***
***Drummond Community High School***

## THE BEACH

The day is bright,
And the wind
Blows calmly.
The sea is calm
And the sand
Bright as the sun
Glows like gold.
The children
Played with buckets and spades
While parents lie down
And sunbathe.
The rocks shine
Bright as ever.
The sun shines brightly.
It is like a ball on fire
That keeps burning.
Then the sea washes
Against the rocks
And big waves
Sneak onto the sand.
The kids start to play
In the water
Which is cold as ice
But no matter
The day is bright
And the wind
Blows calmly.

***Satveer Singh (13)***
***Drummond Community High School***

## TWO VIEWS

I woke up at the edge of dawn
I walk to my balcony.
The blazing sun glares on the calm sea.
The air fresh and a gentle breeze
Blowing my hair away from my face.
Seagulls fly past overhead.
The water is clear and sky blue.
I see the gentle flow of waves.
I watch the spectacular view.
The sun flaming above its reflection
On the clear blue water.
I continue to watch the eye-catching view
Until daylight arrives.
Not a sound is heard
Apart from the cries of seagulls
And the tide lapping in and out
But now midnight has come in.
The water is rough
Murky high waves
In full power crash against
The steep sharp-edged rocks.
On the seashore lie piles of seaweed
And pieces of sharp shells,
Underneath the dark deep
Polluted sea lurk jellyfish.
Huge grey clouds gather together
Filling the sky.

***Kezban Bozkurt (16)***
***Drummond Community High School***

## WINDOW OF MY WORLD

This morning I watched
The cold blue sky
And the sunlight glimmering through
The Scott monument.
Historical, but like a jagged twig,
Sharp to my eye.
The castle high on its rock
Hidden from the crowd.
Peaceful and quiet up there,
Unlike down here so crowded and loud
But when dark starts to fall
The lights glitter on.

People are still around.
The darkness of silence
Cannot stop them,
Racing and pushing,
Talking and shouting.
There is no peace
But there is no anger.
No blood is seen here
Just a long quiet garden
Across from a busy street
Separated like two worlds
The garden still and dark,
The street jumpy and light.

The garden has its peace
Till light comes in.
Then that world
Will too be busy and jumpy.
The people choose their side,
The choice is theirs.

***Nicola Wilson (15)***
***Drummond Community High School***

## In The Cemetery

In the cemetery I stood there,
with my family.
Seeing my uncle being laid to rest,
my eyes full of tears.
Dropping my head,
I took a hold of one of the ropes,
Slowly
lowering the coffin,
Until it touched the bottom.
There was a moment of silence.
I looked around me -
my mum and granny crying.
I moved back away from
the coffin
to comfort them.
Wiping my tears
on my blazer arm.
The men nearby with
shovels and spades
lifted the earth
and threw it onto the coffin.

***Marc Vafaie (16)***
***Drummond Community High School***

## The Night Sky

The sky is pitch black
With the big white moon
That shines so bright.
The stars that sparkle in your eyes,
They make everything shine beautifully
And they stay there all night.

***Louise Goonewardena (12)***
***Drummond Community High School***

## FRIENDS

Friends are fun.
You can share
your thoughts
with them.

Some of my friends
like the same things I like,
so I can talk to
them about that too!

My friends are always
there when I need them.
I can tell them my secrets
and they tell me theirs.

I like the way
my friends
dress.

My friends and I
are all
different.

In some sort of way
we have all picked up
each other's habits.
Love, likes or hates.

If it wasn't for my
friends
I would be totally different!

Who knows what I'd
do without my
*Friends!*

***Rachel Henderson (12)***
***Drummond Community High School***

## WINTERTIME

In the winter
Snow falling from the cloudy sky.
Children building snowmen
Clashing and crunching,
Cold
Because the winter is here.

The best part of wintertime
Christmas
Presents and Christmas trees
Celebrating the birth of the baby Jesus.

Carol songs and singers
In wintertime
With the white trees swaying
It's so great
That wintertime is here.

***Emma Taylor (12)***
***Drummond Community High School***

## THE BEACH

Every morning I go to the beach
Listen to the waves crash
Against each other
Listen to the water quiver
Look around and see
The water flowing softly.

Pebbles so shiny as if they were gold.
Sand so fast as if you were drowning.
The crabs nipping at your toes
As if it was a sharp needle.

A breeze so delicate to blow
Me asleep
Sun shining on the water
As if there was gold under the water

A dolphin so happy, with movement
A shark so creepy as if you could
not see it
A mermaid so joyful as if it was set free.

***R Barnes (12)***
***Drummond Community High School***

## BARNEY

My cat Barney
Is soft and fluffy.
He eats a lot,
Lots of Whiskas cat food.
He goes outside
And chases his tail
And rolls on the ground.
Then at night
He sits beside me,
Moving around on my legs,
And when I'm in bed,
He purrs
And fidgets on top of me,
And in the morning
He wakes me up
By biting my toes
And then he does it all again!

***Jordan Burgess (12)***
***Drummond Community High School***

## THE HEARTACHE

The hurt
The heartache since you left
The wanting your presence once again
The longing for your tender care
Holding me tight
And expressing your love.

The night you left
Did you know you took my heart
Bruised and torn
You left with her - my 'best friend'
Deceit
And betrayal by both my loved ones . . .

I remember the time
We went out with her
We arrived first
And you left the room
What I want to know
Is were you with her?

They say 'love is blind'
But is that just to cover
The stupidity
Of someone in love
I should have seen it coming
But I was too naive
To admit to it happening.

But I wish you well
in your new life.
I hope you are happy
And contented with her.
Or is it all a game
You like to play
With people's emotions?

Is it the satisfaction
That you enjoy?
Because if you're not careful
You will end up alone
Because we'll have grown wise
To your game
And
No longer wish
To play . . .

***Michelle Bolochowekyj (15)***
***Drummond Community High School***

## NATURE

Sitting calmly
Staring out the window
I see green trees
I hear singing birds
And a bright blue sky.
A shining yellow sun
Dazzles my eyes.
Everything is quiet
Except for the whistling of the birds
And the gentle swaying of the trees.
Soft, fluffy clouds
Are scattered about the sky.
They float above my head
Like giant bits of candyfloss.

***John Martin (12)***
***Drummond Community High School***

## UFO

As he creeps through the trees,
Agent Mulder starts to see
A distant light,
Very bright.
As he gets nearer
The scene becomes clearer,
A crashed UFO,
People rush to and fro,
Trying to clear up the mess,
Before people start to guess
Because if they find out
Their safety they'll doubt.
A toxic chemical spill?
It fits the bill.
A man gives the orders,
To 'Close all the borders'
To avoid 'contamination'
Mulder watches in fascination.
Remembers his camera and in a trice,
Clicks the button once or twice.
He had to admit he got quite a good piccy,
He thought this'll stop Scully from taking the mickey.
But as he imagined the look on her face,
A guy in a suit saw him and gave chase.
But Mulder's foot had got wedged between stones
So he just sat on the ground and groaned
And when he was in isolation,
They took away his consolation.
When his camera was gone he miserably swore,
Looking for aliens really was a bore!

***Lizy Smith (13)***
***Drummond Community High School***

## My First Pet

My first pet
was a hamster.
I fed him grapes
To see his cheeks puff up.
He looked so cute.
Sometimes I would let him run
Through . . . my . . . sleeve!
I thought it was tickly.

But when he got old,
He would cuddle into me
And he would sniff my face
And lick it.
I really loved Bobby.
He meant a lot to me.

At night I would take
His cage into my room.
I'd take him and sing for him.
He loved me singing to him.

I would usually put him
To sleep
And he enjoyed it.

When he died I was crying.
I buried him in the back green
And my dad got me another one.
So I called it Bobby too.

***Michelle Cunnison (11)***
***Drummond Community High School***

## People In The Town

This morning I watched from my window
The sun shining onto the gardens and the castle
Seeing the trees swaying in the warm breeze
People shopping and people sunbathing
People climbing the Scott Monument like climbing
A tall mountain with a great view.

But is it?
You look out on one side you see
The castle, the gardens, all the people having fun.
Then you look at the other side -
You still see the people.
People shopping with all their money.
Getting new clothes and necessary utensils.
But if you look through all that you see
People sitting in doorways of shops
Sitting with a hat in front
With pennies in it.

Homelessness is something which happens to you
Homelessness isn't something you choose to happen
To you.
It just happens.

***Simone Martin (14)***
***Drummond Community High School***

## The Witch That Flies

The witch that flies in the night,
*Help* what a terrible sight,
Her feet are smelly as a skunk,
Eyes that are like the moon,
There's going to be some screaming soon.

Her hair is thin and like straw,
Nose as warty as a toad,
Her back is like a camel's hump,
Her broom is as thin as her legs,
She has hands like pegs,
*Zzoomm* and off she goes.

***Mark McKeown (12)***
***Firrhill High School***

## THE WITCH'S MONEY SPELL

The leg of a toad,
Crushed on the road.
Fox's head,
A nanny goat's leg.
A pig's liver,
It will make you shiver.
A twig of a tree,
Cut off by me.
Lots of slime,
The money will be mine.
Mix it up well
And say the spell.
Make me money
And don't be funny.
I want millions,
Billions trillions.
The money will come true,
But I'll not give any to you.

***Alan Mackay (12)***
***Firrhill High School***

## THE WITCHES

''Tis midnight' cried the witches.
'Time to make our spell.'
They ran towards the cauldron,
One said 'Let's make everyone unwell.'

Another said 'Oh no let's raise them from the dead'
They cackled out loud a lot
But one shook her head
'We really need a good thought'

'But what can we do?'
'I know let's make all cows bark
And all dogs moo.'
This time they thought oh what a lark.

They put in the ingredients
They even sang a song
Can you guess what happened next?
It all went wrong.

Instead the witches started to miaow
The black cat started talking
The witches are down on hands and knees
And guess what, the cat is walking.

***Lynn McGrail (12)***
***Firrhill High School***

## WANDS

A wand is magic
Very very magic
It can do good and bad things
It changes people into things
Things that they would rather not be
Witches normally have wands
The one that I saw did.

I saw a scary ugly witch
She had a wand that was
Black with yellow spots
I was scared I was shaking in my shoes
Of the very very scary ugly witch
She cast a spell on me
It didn't work I got away.

***Steven McGowan (11)***
***Firrhill High School***

## WITCH OF LAGOON

Only on a full moon
Does the witch from the lagoon
Pop out to cause a riot
For her dinner of delight
She brings her cauldron
All the time
To mix an ugly slime
She says in her cauldron
Mix a spell so bad that it will kill
All pretty girls
'Snakes, frogs and cats' tails
All whirl ghosts' nails
I'll send a ghost to
The town so that
It is broken down
Ha Ha
Hear me cry
I'll be back to make you die.'

***Fiona Dickson (12)***
***Firrhill High School***

## THE ENCHANTED FOREST

I walk through the forest
It's getting darker every minute.
'Twoo Twoo'
'What's that?' I cry.
I spin round to see two *big* yellow eyes
Staring at me!
It's only an owl!

I keep walking, scared stiff.
I'm all alone.
I think that's why I feel watched.
'Whistle, whistle'
I jump out of my skin
And then I realise it's only the wind.

All around me I see darkness.
I feel mystified by the silence broken by me
Cracking the twigs as I step on them.

***Evelyn Henney (12)***
***Firrhill High School***

## NOSELESS WITCH

Imagine being a witch
Who hasn't got a nose
The only thing I got
Is a golf ball size mole

I tried to cast a spell
To make me have a nose
The only thing I've got
Was hairs upon my mole

I said the spell again
Clickity clop swish swash
Make me have a nose
*Boom!*

My forehead has a nose
And not above my mouth
Now my fringe gets in my way
When I have to pick it out.

***Melina Walker (12)***
***Firrhill High School***

## THE WITCH'S CASTLE

Up on a big dark hill!
Lived there witches.
In their big big castle
With the little black cat.

In the big big black castle's dungeon,
There was a black cauldron
With a big spoon to stir it,
The three witches started a spell.

'Hocus pocus alacazam,'
They chanted,
We shall turn all humans into sand.
They chanted again,
Dancing round the cauldron,
The witches' faces turned green
They disappeared with a poof.
They cast a spell on themselves.

***Michael Davis (12)***
***Firrhill High School***

## The Pretty People Spell

This spell makes you look pretty
And makes all your friends look gritty

First you go down to Boots
And buy some dye to cover your roots.
Then you pour it in a bowl
And boil it on top of some coal.

This spell makes you look pretty
And makes all your friends look gritty.

Then you get all your friends' looks
So you seem a pretty good cook.
Now you mix it up in one
So it weighs a very big tonne.

This spell makes you look pretty
And makes all your friends look gritty.

Get all your best make-up
Throw it in a pot
And turn up the heat
And make it steam a lot.

This spell makes you look pretty
And makes all your friends look gritty.

Now you have a potion for prettiness.
Let's just hope it brings you happiness.

This spell makes you look pretty
And makes all your friends look gritty.

***Gemma Carnie (12)***
***Firrhill High School***

## A Witch

A witch has eyes as black as death,
The nose and the mouth are a terrible mess.
She looks around her dim grey world,
Looking for you for she wants her dinner
And if she finds you she'll plump you up
With chicken and chocolate you'll soon be full up.
First she'll rip your leg off,
This will be a nice munch for brunch,
Then she will take the other and save it for later.
The stomach, lungs and liver make a nice stew for dinner.
Then comes her supper the brain and the bladder
And your hair will be useful for killing the next victim.

***Iain McMichael (12)***
***Firrhill High School***

## Snap Snap Snap You Little Trap

I have a wish to be rich
This funny old witch said
'You, little woman, may I grant your wish?'
'Yes please.' 'Snap your fingers and
Your wish will come true.'
My little wish makes me snap
I feel so happy
Snap snap snap
I crack my teeth so hard
Maybe I wish to be rich too much.
So snap snap snap
All the way down to the funny old road.

***Claire Connor (12)***
***Firrhill High School***

## TALKING CAT

My best friend Sammy
Went into this house,
She came out with a big shout.

She said 'There's a cat,
A talking talking cat.'
I spoke 'I don't believe you.'
She mumbled 'There is, come with me.'

We went to explore
With a knock at the door.
Then in the back of
The black room became a
Cat, a black cat.

He started to speak,
I thought it was weird.
I was full of shock
He said 'Please get down
On your knees and sneeze on me.'

The spell was broken,
We became friends,
Just like it used to be.

***Siobhan Wells (12)***
***Firrhill High School***

## WITCHES

Witches witches have creaky voices
Ugly faces and pointy noses.
They have black cats and crooked hats and
Black baggy dresses and
They fly on old straw brooms.

Witches have cauldrons with mixed frogs
And snakes and other horrible things.
If you don't watch out they might give you a fright
Or put a spell on you and turn you into
A cow or a pig or a horse or even a frog.
You might even have to be kissed by a prince.

***Jennifer Hamilton (11)***
***Firrhill High School***

## ENCHANTING POWER

Darkness falls yet again,
Gloom and doom in the atmosphere.
Elves and dwarves scurry around the town square,
Screams and shrieks everywhere.

Lightning strikes terror,
People cursed and doomed forever.
Up, up high in the tower,
Lives a man of enchanting power.
The wizard wise,
By cauldron bubble,
To take over town of trouble.

The moon is hazy,
Not bringing light,
Stories and tales of terror and fright.

Back in the tower,
He casts a spell,
A secret untold and still not to tell.
The tower shaking,
Wizard falls to the ground.
The tower crumbles,
A crash a bang, silence no sound!

***Annika Ramirez (12)***
***Firrhill High School***

## ORBIT EXPLOSION

Flickering light
In a cold, dark room,
Witches round a cauldron
Mixing with a spoon.
Bubbles rising up and up,
Cackling aplenty, it never stops.

The witch's black cat
Emerged from behind a door.
It began to walk closer and closer
To the cackling witches behind the fire.
Suddenly it stopped.
The black cat had jumped onto the pot.

Crashing and banging,
The cat fell in the fire.
'Burned to a frazzle'
The witches cried and cried,
As the smoke grew higher and higher,
There was a huge explosion from the fire.

Flying colours went across the room.
The booming explosion
Sent the witches out of the room.
Across the black sky
And into orbit, across to Mars
Never to come back, I wonder why?

***Elizabeth Muirhead (11)***
***Firrhill High School***

## WEIRDO FAMILY

My Aunt Hagatha's a really nice witch
She has a black hat
And a stripy ginger cat
She has strange and old friends
Who scare me a lot
My Aunt Hagatha's a really nice witch

My Uncle Harry's a really horrid ghoul
His dark, dank hole is no place for a fool
His girlfriend is a ghost
His daughter is a troll
My Uncle Harry's a really horrid ghoul

My sister is an elf, a really weird elf
She lives up a tree
And comes down on Hallows Eve
She has a boyfriend too
He's a pixie through and through
My sister is an elf a really weird elf

As you can see
I have a weirdo family
But I am normal
Believe me, I am
*Normal!*

***Claire Ford (12)***
***Firrhill High School***

## THE BLACK CAT

The black cat, he's evil,
He's slim and sleek, he's dark and black,
And never forget he's wild,
The black cat!

The black cat, he's daring,
He uses the witch's hat,
And the broom and the cauldron,
The black cat!

The black cat, he doesn't feel good,
After he used the witch's hat again,
'Cause he was caught and turned into a frog,
The black cat!

The black cat, he's green,
But he needed to be a cat again,
So he got the witch's spell book, used a spell, and now,
He's the black cat again!

***Jonathan Dick (12)***
***Firrhill High School***

## I KNOW A WITCH . . .

I know a witch
Her name is Sarah.
She lives in a castle
And does spells all day.

I know a witch
Her name is Sarah.
She has a cat his name is Sallim.
He's the cat that never shuts up.

I know a witch
Her name is Sarah.
She has a dog but it could be a frog.

I know a witch
Her name is Sarah.
Ooops, I'm looking in the mirror.

***Angela Lonnie (12)***
***Firrhill High School***

## THE THREE WITCHES

Once there were three witches
Who lived upon a hill.
They lived in a castle,
And one witch was ill.

They were very happy,
Until one sunny day.
Five men came to visit,
To modernise the place.

The witches were finding life
Hard enough, especially
The witch who was ill.
They tried all their spells,
But none of them worked well.

They called the national witches' line,
Who sent the world's best witch.
She cast a spell
That scared the men,
And left the leader dead.

***Michael Knott (11)***
***Firrhill High School***

## Bill (The Cyclops)

There is a Cyclops named Bill,
Who is a cannibal.
Now Bill lived in a cave
On a hill in a place in Portugal.

Originally Bill came from Italy
So he ate lots of pizza for tea -
(Maybe the odd human refugee!)

Bill always did enjoy cooking,
But he really got angry looking
For his Delia Smith cook book!

He looked as far as he could
But truly that did no good.
He looked high and low
He looked far and wide -
Who knows where the cook book
Could have went to hide?

Bill went to his friend called Lill
For an aspirin pill, and told Lill
His great tale about his book,
And his great look.

Lill made a cup of tea
And what do you know -
What did she see
A Delia Smith cook book, oh glee!

Bill was so happy he jumped up with joy
And started an earthquake the bad little boy
(Cyclops even!)
When he got home he made pizza for tea
'Cause he's Bill the Cyclops you see!

***Lochlan McGarr (11)***
***Firrhill High School***

## Black Magic

There once was a witch
Who lived in a ditch
She was soon to be hitched to Mitch
He was rich!

There once was a goblin who did have a problem
His knees were always knobblin'
So he went to Robin another goblin and he cured him
And no more was he wobblin'!

There once was a wizard who was
Always in a dizzard.
So he went outside
And got caught in a blizzard!

A happy ending (maybe).

***Aimee Jones (12)***
***Firrhill High School***

## Hocus Pocus

Looking at our spell book,
What shall we cook,
An old man's finger,
Or a bad old crook.
Let us cook the crook,
And the old man's finger,
Now the mixture's done,
We'll fix the spell together.
Hocus Pocus make this potion
Into body lotion.

***Madelaine Stuart (12)***
***Firrhill High School***

## Spellbound!

Power, magic, potions and spells,
Bad witchcraft and witches,
Dancing, chanting, riding broomsticks,
Scary, haunting they may be.

Happiness, joy, kind, helpful,
Good witches and witchcraft,
Magic, dancing spells, bright light,
Cheerful, lovely they may be.

Witches witches,
Thought of as ugly horrible dark figures,
Witches witches,
Never thought of as good kind bright figures.

***Laura McHarry (11)***
***Firrhill High School***

## Rainbows

Rainbows are magic,
Rainbows are colourful,
Rainbows are everything,
Everything but horrible.

Rainbows are red,
Yellow and blue,
Rainbows are doubles,
You sometimes find two!

Rainbows are glittery,
Rainbows are stars,
Rainbows are lovely,
Just like Mars bars!

***Gemma Bell (12)***
***Firrhill High School***

## Footsteps

Footsteps
I hear footsteps
Silence
They've gone

Creaking of floorboards
Scurrying of mice
Windows banging
Footsteps

Wicked laughs
Lots of them
Bubbling
Boiling
Footsteps

Footsteps getting louder
Getting near
Creaking coming closer
Where are they coming from?

The cellar
It's coming from the cellar
Witches
Witches in my cellar

I knew the house was haunted
I was right
No one would believe me
I was right.

***Laura Syme (12)***
***Firrhill High School***

## The Ocean

The ocean is so full,
But full of what?
It cannot be explained,
There are too many mysteries.

The ocean is hiding secrets,
Dark, creepy secrets.
I think it yearns to tell us,
In its huge, crashing waves.

The ocean is so beautiful,
With its dark, deep blue,
It is like a close friend,
Swishing on the beach.

The ocean is so hypnotic,
As the tide goes in and out,
The ocean can keep me spellbound,
For long endless hours.

***Kirsty Fairhead (11)***
***Firrhill High School***

## Witches And Warlocks

I mix my magic
To make a ghost.
I mix in a dragon a toad and a bat.
I wiggle my bum Boom!

I'm melting . . . melting . . .
I'm a *ghost.*
Oh no I am a silly stupid ghost.
What will my daddy say?

I hope he won't see me,
What if he does see me?
I'll be in trouble,
Then I'll go to the devils.

***Neil Leitch (12)***
***Firrhill High School***

## SPELLBOUND!

Frightened, spooked, dazzled, excited
All kinds of magic makes me feel this way
Evil, good, horrid and happy
Different magic, all these kinds.

Witches, goblins, wizards, warlocks
Plot against me in every way
Venom of snake, toe of frog
Eye of newt and tongue of dog
As they danced that was what they said

I'm enthralled, entranced and stunned
This is what their chant has done
I cannot move, I'm in their power
I'm worried, confused at the top of their tower

Relieved, pleased, glad, happy
I broke through and stole their wand
They all melt
I say goodbye
That's the last of them I happily sigh.

Sitting at home, telling my story
Everyone's shaking their head
They won't believe me, no one will
But just this once I'm right!

***Allison McIntosh (12)***
***Firrhill High School***

## THE APPRENTICE

I was looking for a job in the newspaper the 'Daily Din'
It said 'Apprentice needed for evil warlock, apply within'
I said 'That sounds like a job that would really interest me'
But then I didn't know what the consequences would be.

I went to the place it told me on top of Haunted Hill
It was no house nor a flat but a great big old castle
I went and knocked on the door and I heard a voice say
'Come in please'
This wasn't the only thing knocking, so were my knees.

I liked the job at the start, getting stuff really clean
Doing odd jobs, polishing, you know what I mean
But then it got a real big pain
He told me to collect some weird stuff, including brains.

I went into his lab one night
Some things in there gave me a fright
But then the warlock saw me and he grabbed a knife
And I ran and ran and ran and ran for my life.

I ran down Haunted Hill deep into the forest
I could feel my heart pounding in my chest
Then I tripped upon a log
He caught up with me and turned me into a frog.

Things aren't going bad right now I can jump really high
And when I get hungry, I can eat some flies
If you want to see me, come down to Stimpsons pond
If you listen carefully you'll hear me ribbeting my song.

***Scott Jones (12)***
***Firrhill High School***

## Magic Calculator

I picked it up
Coming home from school
A hexagon calculator
Shiny and blue
Letter buttons on it too.

A note was stuck on the back
Giving me instructions
The little calcu will do
Anything I want it to
It just peeps down
At my page and does
My maths 1 2 3!

I sailed through maths
Until one day when
We had a test and
I could not use
My clever little calcu
I did so awfully
Two marks out of fifty.

Now I've learnt
My lesson true
I'll never ever cheat again
As for my little clever calcu
Thrown away down the loo!

***Eilidh Webster (12)***
***Firrhill High School***

## The Fairy

I'm an upset fairy
I don't know why.
My life is misery
I can't fly.
I can't sing or dance
I only want a chance.
I'm not allowed a wand
I feel like jumping in a pond.
But now I'm happy
That I talked things through.
I guess I'm happy
For me and you!

***Patricia Chirnside (12)***
***Firrhill High School***

## The Future

Some of us claim we can see into the future,
Some of us are scared of what it brings,
Some of us await its coming with
excitement and happiness,
Every second, we move into the future,
Never to return to the past,
But, no matter how much we will it come,
or wish it stay away,
There is nothing we can do about it,
As the future comes and we go by,
We cannot stop its happening,
As the future's always coming.

***Lydia Papandrianou (12)***
***George Heriot's School***

## Love

Love,
Cherished and held,
By all who love thee.
Lush forests, soothing oceans,
Beckoning, 'Marry me.'
The wind is howling,
Stripping off your leaves,
Leaving you worshipped by the sun,
No shivering knees.
When weak from starvation,
Strong arms, warm to the touch.
Fall into dreams,
It is too much.
When bitter cold reaches its peak,
You have no choice, but to die,
Let love carry you away,
Above the freeze you will fly.
The scent of sweet musk roses,
The fiery passion in a soul.
Radiant beauty of a stranger,
Down the hills you will roll.
The moon blesses its light onto the land,
It resembles an orient pearl,
Wrapping you in its delicate rays,
Wondrous feelings linger, boy or girl.
Love.

***Vinaya Jigajinni (13)***
***George Heriot's School***

## THE SEA HORSE

*Walk* - The horse is now calm and content,
But soon the waves will not relent.
The sea's pace is very steady,
It seems as though the breakers are ready.

*Trot* - You will hear the horse neigh,
When she decides that the waves should come out to play.
The horse's pace is now quite brisk,
Will she decide to take the risk?

*Canter* - The waves are now getting increasingly violent,
The horse's hooves are completely silent.
As the wind blows you can hear the horse sigh.
The waves are now extremely high.

*Gallop* - Tossed mane and tail in the air,
The sea gallops everywhere.
This wild beast cannot be tamed.
She belongs to no one she cannot be claimed.

***Naomi Pryde (12)***
***George Heriot's School***

## THE SUMMER'S OUT

The fields quivering, the skyline a grimace,
Another harvest gathered in,
The swallow of summer, the barbed harpoon,
White, ivory while among the rambling greens.
With a dusky gold that filled the pond beside the road,
Beneath those rugged elms, that yew tree's shade.
Had stepped before me to the water's edge,
Now high and dry, dead in the willow herb.

***Sophie Read (12)***
***George Heriot's School***

## London Rooftops

All I dream,
Is to stand,
Upon the rooftops of London.

Early in the morning,
As the city wakes up,
Or late in the evening,
As the city goes to sleep.

I dream of standing there,
All alone,
With nobody but the birds
And gaze at the glorious skyline,
From the rooftops of London.

To see the street lamps flickering,
To hear the chimes of Big Ben,
To smell the chimney smoke,
To taste the drizzling rain,
From the rooftops of London,
Is a heart-warming feeling.

The red buses file past,
The cathedral doors open,
The river streaming by,
The picture sellers at the park,
The tourists outside the palace,
The Londoners on the go,
Is what I long to see, from the rooftops one day.

To stand there is a dream,
That one day will be fulfilled,
Then alone, the streets I will stroll,
And know I have seen the world,
From the rooftops of London.

***Laura Marquis (12)***
***George Heriot's School***

## ENOUGH FEELING

The rain falls like liquid silver
On the floodlit fountain
Bright and lovely in the darkness;
Summer music
Relaxed and high
Rises above the kiss.

The wild grass
Spring green and free.
The Earth, the creatures, the laughter,
The love.
Go, now, go!

People dance feeling the storm
The right party flies by
And the years you and me
Laughed in the brilliant world.
The scent of honey new and pure
Escapes life now.

***Megan McKrell (13)***
***George Heriot's School***

## SNOW

'Cor, it's snowing!'
Endless possibilities in the untouched world.
Frigid fingers form lakes and mountains
As snow is scooped and thrown joyously.
Boys like new puppies roll and scamper,
Scrape knees and elbows on new-made slides.
Battle lines form, disband, regroup
As snowballs find their targets.
Laughter rings out as they jostle and shove
Together.

'Oh dear, it's snowing!'
She sits quietly cradling her cup of tea.
Her walk to the village is now out of the question.
Broken ankle, broken hip, hypothermia -
Too dreadful to contemplate.
No visitors today either.
She turns from the immaculate landscape
To her immaculate room
And contemplates her prison
Alone.

***Helen Pratt (13)***
***George Heriot's School***

## The Romantic Question

I saw you standing,
Your smile, so wide,
I stared at you lovingly,
Your hair an ebb tide.
You were catching my glance,
I turned away in shame,
You walked over slowly,
'Excuse me, what's your name?'
Something in the way you spoke
The smooth sweet sound,
It filled my head and stayed there,
Going round and round and round.
'Jo,' I replied, taking my time,
I blushed and bowed my head,
I asked 'And yours?'
He smiled, 'Jacob' he said.

***Susan Jack (12)***
***George Heriot's School***

## A Close Moment

Above the midden rose the sun,
Those late November days.
The morning sky stretched pale and cold,
And from the east night clouds unfold.

The crunch of boots on gravelled walk,
The quiet stir of frosted leaves,
The lonely bark of calling fox.
The distant baaing of farmers' flocks.

A horse stood out in the stable yard,
Her head held high for she was proud.
She stood beside the wooden gate,
In trust that I was never late.

I turned the lock, pushed open the door,
She followed me closely at my side.
Her breath was warm around my arm,
Her ears pricked up for sound of alarm.

The steaming bucket of oats and molasses,
Heady smells of bran and peelings,
She plunges deep into her feed,
And chomps away with happy greed.

***Sebastian Collins (14)***
***George Heriot's School***

## Hello, My Friend

Oh hello my little friend
What news do you send
Is it about spring?
Is that why you sing?

Have you found a nest?
A cosy place to rest
Take care my little sweet
I hope some day again we'll meet.

***Aimee McLaughlin (13)***
***George Heriot's School***

## THE FARM

The farmyard is silent,
There isn't a sound,
Everyone is sleeping,
Even the worms in the ground.

The cock crows, harmonically,
Waking everyone at dawn,
The people get up,
Without even a yawn.

The people have breakfast,
The animals are fed,
The farmer gets his tools.

The children are playing,
The lambs are gambolling,
Everyone keeps to the rules.

Life on a farm is different by far,
Nobody comes to any harm,
If I got to choose my ideal home,
I definitely would live on a farm.

***Jenny Williams (12)***
***George Heriot's School***

## Hope

Who am I to talk of life?
Of it I've had so little.
But what I know is truly that it comes and goes
Death
Life
Not same, not different, just there
I've known both.
It's strange a lifetime of both until one halts.
You try to turn back, to fully understand.
Yet you can't.
You can only hope to see them again some day . . .

***Nicole Brandon (12)***
***George Heriot's School***

## Conservation

*C* onservation means save our Earth,
*O* nly you and I can help.
*N* ever say it's far too hard,
*S* imple things will make the difference.
*E veryone* can help our cause,
*R* eady to start?
*V* ery soon our work will be done . . .
*A* nd a clean and glorious Earth will await,
*T* hose who help to conserve her.
*I* n our old and polluted world . . .
*O* nly now will pollution go
N ever to return.

***Michael A Wilson (12)***
***George Heriot's School***

## My Special Dream

A memory I have from my childhood years
Is a dream I'll not forget
A thought, a hobby, a thing I loved
Even now it lingers yet.

We were cantering in the hills
My chestnut mare and I
The morning sun was shining
Through an untroubled sky.

The only company we had
Was the wind, the flowers, the trees
Rabbits around my horse's hooves
Playing in scattered leaves.

As we got faster and faster
The wind was blowing my hair
Alone we raced through the valley
We are such a perfect pair.

The lovely glorious feeling
Of being away together
Passing tree trunks and ditches
Riding through deep purple heather.

And then we broke into a gallop
As we jumped a bubbling stream
The sensational feeling of flying
It's a shame it's only a dream.

***Jennifer Liddell (13)***
***George Heriot's School***

## The Sea

As I walk my heart along the swaying shores of the kingdom of blue,
The gulls searching, swooping along the edge of the sand cry and call
out for joy as they are in the ever-silent heaven of enchantment,
Seaweed, rich in green and purple, disperses, gliding along in a
transparent film of wave along the tide,
Gems of the sea, round, curled, oval, wait on the sand for the next tide
to give them a ride,
For the blue is the centre of the soul,
As a fairytale ship casts its footprints of wave across the horizon,
Volleys of white crash and withdraw on its bow, the same spray
that is smashing into the rocks at the far end of the beach,
out of the spray comes all the miscellaneous of the deep, the natural
rejects of whatever the sea doesn't like, starfish glinting in the sun,
dead, but finding new life among the new creatures of the sand,
Also all the human debris, an old shoe, torn and riddled with sand,
A glass bottle housing a host of seaweed.
If you walk along to the rocks you can see the fishermen
old and tired, with rods in their hands, looking into the great beyond.
After all the sea is a great beyond,
Never ceasing to be great.

***Douglas Maxwell (11)***
***George Heriot's School***

## Maybe It's Not Enough

Son against father,
Daughter against mother,
Is this what we need to make the real
and shining new world?

Two forces converging together,
This causes the old and new forever,
Forever over and over in one mind
and one blood.

One body loves another,
Wonder what they'd do without each other,
Every moment we all pray that
love truly is all we need.

***India Phillips (13)***
***George Heriot's School***

## ANIMALS

Elephants!
One of the *largest* mammals around,
Stomping and stamping, with eyes of gold that glow,
Snacking on a little bamboo as they go.

Lions!
One of the most *ferocious* animals,
Sly and sleek as they hunt their prey,
They'll eat anything which comes their way.

Bears!
One of the more *woolly* animals,
Although, get on their wrong side, they'll bite
They won't if you stand still and don't fight.

Camels!
Definitely the *bumpiest* of animals,
Desert animals unless kept in zoos,
Their humps of course usually come in twos.

Kangaroos!
One of the *jumpier* animals,
Hopping around with their babies in pouch,
They're certainly bouncy, for that I can vouch!

***Casey Nicol (12)***
***George Heriot's School***

## MOLE

Deep under your lawn, who's hiding, can you guess?
His coat is dark and silky smooth,
But don't be led astray,
Underneath this friendly cover, he is searching out
his prey.
He's powered by a desire to finish off all grubs,
But while he's trying to help himself, he is mining
through our tubs.

Deep under your lawn, can you guess who's there?
Tunnelling and burrowing, he works by touch not sight,
Living deep below the ground he digs and digs
all night
Hearing very little, oblivious to all
But, beware all wriggling creatures, should you,
perchance, to fall.

Deep, under your lawn, guess who's waiting?
Waiting for a worm,
Ah! Here one comes with a squiggle and a squirm.
In a cascade of earth he lands in his path,
And *scrunch!*
It's Mr Mole's lunch!

***Katie Simpson (12)***
***George Heriot's School***

## STALKERS

They come together,
In search of food,
Foxes, badgers and moles.
They raid the bins,
And leave the scraps,
Then scuttle away,
While the gardener naps.

Lumps in the grass,
Turned-up soil,
Such annoying creatures.
They suck down the daisies,
Tulips and mum's plants,
Destroying the
Garden's features.

***Jackie Young (12)***
***George Heriot's School***

## THE FIRST DAY

I walked briskly in my crisp kilt and stiff new blazer,
My feet clicked against the tarmac.
The winding path seemed to last forever.
As I approached the playground I slowed down,
I took a deep breath and looked up,
The playground was packed full.
Everybody in groups, talking and laughing,
At ease with their friends.
I weaved myself between the crowds,
Like a minnow through a sea of sharks.
I headed towards the building I had marked on my school map.
Cautiously I climbed the stairs,
Checking the room numbers as I went.
Thinking of what my class would be like,
Whether or not I would enjoy myself here.
One - three - nine,
One - four - two,
There it was, one - four - four.
I hesitated again.
Stepped up the last step and reached for the doorknob.

***Danielle Young (14)***
***George Heriot's School***

## If We Could Look . . .

Far in the future, what will be?
If we could look, what would we see?
New technology, robots, aliens,
Peace, war, a paradise, a hell
Who can tell?

Back in the past, in BC,
What was there?
If we could look, what would we see?
Plains, oceans, deserts,
Dinosaurs, plants, primitive man?
Who knows?

If we could look at ourselves,
What would we see?
Death, greed, war,
New technology, bigger guns, better bombs,
A world divided, a primitive race,
That's what we'd see.

***Stephen Welsh (12)***
***George Heriot's School***

## Blob!

From where it had come,
No one could guess.
'Twas harder to explain,
Than the monster of Loch Ness.

The difference was,
He could often be seen.
An enormous great blob,
That glowed bright green.

The blob became angry,
And also rather sad.
Then it perked up,
And seemed to go mad.

Then a new blob arrived,
A lady-like pink one.
They made baby blobs,
Who played in the sun

*And had fun . . .*

***Luke Jones ((12)***
***George Heriot's School***

## THE STRAWBERRY SUNDAE

I remember saying 'Wow,'
Today I say 'Danke mein Frau.'
It was the biggest ice-cream I'd ever seen,
'Is this from the children's menu?' I asked.

The dish was full of strawberries and ice-cream
Perhaps smaller fruits, perhaps smaller scoops,
The spoon had a big, long handle,
This spoon has a long handle,
'Granddad, do you want some of mine?'
Just a snack, 'Mum, have you finished your coffee yet?'

The boy at the next table just said 'Wow!'
Wonder what he'll say, seven years from now.

***Joanne Collings (14)***
***George Heriot's School***

## NIGHT

As a child looking out of the window,
I see things that fascinate and enthral.
But the time of day that captures my interest,
Is the time unseen by all.

Like a curtain of darkness being drawn,
Over a lively room of colour.
Night-time opens a door to more life,
Life that is ignored in each darkened hour.

The nocturnal species of foxes,
Timid and humble wild pheasant.
Badgers and bats with only victuals on their mind,
Cats on the prowl, eyes incandescent.

Rustling and scratching is heard from the window,
Cooing and twittering from birds.
Flapping and fluttering of wings in the bushes,
The wind whispers softly like spoken words.

There is so much more to discover,
About life in the hours of twilight.
Still I will keep on observing though
And get all my rest during daylight!

***Katie Bannister (11)***
***George Heriot's School***

## TOAD

I stared out of the window,
past the sheets of rain
that were filling my garden,
and laid my eyes upon the creature.

He had been there long,
studying the jungles of flowers,
waiting for his next meal to arrive,
whilst enjoying the droplets of water
descending from his green coat.

He became aware of my presence,
and as my arm fell,
his eyes glared at me
and he sat motionless.

Suddenly filled with excitement
I hurried away to look for a box,
or any contraption that would contain him,
but when I returned he was gone.

Had he read my thoughts
and hastily escaped imprisonment,
leaving me feeling guilty
at the thought of taking away his freedom.

How I longed to see the toad once again.

***Kieran Ferguson (13)***
***George Heriot's School***

## My World

I stand at the boundary of two worlds
with the land behind me and the sea before me.
In the sky there are gulls flying
Like spots of white light in the ever-changing sky
They wheel and soar and look down on me.

Their eerie cries float down from that other world
Where I do not belong like echoes from the past.
I envy them because I am not like them.
Why? Why can't I fly away on my own to see and think
and beauty?
The setting sun reflects on my wet face.

I used to walk through the uni to think.
There were gulls there too; different though -
silently watching from chimney pots.
It was quiet and beautiful and all mine.
But . . . I knew it would happen, like it does every autumn,
every year.

One day the campus wasn't mine anymore.
Signs like 'free' and 'restricted access' filled me with dislike
though it felt good someone shared my ideals.
I got scared - of change and study.
Scared that I could never be like the students.

So I came here.
But here I am jealous because I want to be a bird and fly away.
Back in the uni I wasn't jealous. I liked it there.

Maybe the world behind me isn't that bad . . .
Maybe, maybe it's good.
Work, hate, friends, crowds, love, loneliness . . .
I actually quite like it.
Any life is beautiful in its own way, I think. Any place, any person.

I don't think I feel scared anymore.
And anyway, real life's got Benjie in it.

So I turn away from the gulls; back to the Earth
and I blink back the tears
and get on with it.

Tomorrow I think I'll go through the uni again.

***Stephanie Droop (13)***
***George Heriot's School***

## AUTUMN

Leaves fluttering,
Falling to the ground,
Red, orange, gold,
Hardly making a sound.

Squirrels collecting conkers,
Rabbits hiding in burrows,
All the animals preparing,
For their long winter's sleep.

Children playing amongst the leaves,
Hiding, running,
Throwing, screaming,
Watching the leaves fall down again.

The fireworks pop,
The sky lights up,
Children shouting,
More! More!

The bonfires crackle,
The flames rise high,
More wood put on,
Soon to reach the sky.

***Karen Williamson (12)***
***George Heriot's School***

## Banjo Man

Every time I go to town he's sitting in the street,
Singing songs from years ago, his dog beside his feet.
His music warms the hearts of all that pass him on their way,
But they can't spare the time to say just how well he plays.

At the end of each chorus he shouts 'Good day' and 'Could you spare some change?'
But people just turn their heads away. They've got their own lives to arrange.
They walk on by without a care, never turning back.
He's been given a bad name by the people in his pack.

I wonder what is going on
Inside his mind.
How can people be so cruel
to one so talented and kind?

***Liam Upton (11)***
***George Heriot's School***

## Question Time

Why are we here on Planet Earth?
What is our purpose, what is our worth?
Why does a bird fly to highest heights?
Why are there days and why are there nights?
Why are there animals big and small?
An insect so tiny - a giraffe so tall?
Why is there summer and why is there spring?
Why do we dance and why do we sing?
Why is there a world of good things and bad?
Why are we happy and why are we sad?

*Why?*

***Vanessa Garden (12)***
***George Heriot's School***

## Stan

The snow outside is falling hard now,
But my cousin's too busy to notice.
The remainders of the Christmas party are nearly gone,
Another Christmas through with.

But this year the tree will be taken down early,
And the presents played with less.
For this year's not like the others,
For this year Stan's not here.

I never really knew why,
But Stan was always here.
He wasn't part of the family and
He wasn't a very close friend.

But every Christmas, Stan would be here,
Telling stories of battles he'd won.
How he'd sailed the Seven Seas,
And fought pirates with his trusty sword.

He always brought the nicest presents,
For they were just what everybody wanted.
When I was little I remember,
Thinking he was Santa Claus.

But now he is not with us,
Gone to a better place said Mum.
I still think he comes to our house at Christmas,
But quietly so as not to be noticed.

***Kylee Brown (14)***
***George Heriot's School***

## The Hunt

As they rounded the bend they saw it
half-dead eyes glazed
brush hanging limply,
a cry of triumph rose
and the staccato noise of the horn
called out the death sentence
Their breath coming in savage gasps
they flung themselves upon it.
It was ripped and bitten and torn
as it screamed like a child in pain.
'But it needed to be controlled, it was a pest
and the hounds were quick, clean and humane.'
This is what the hunters said
as it lay there dead
and the screams echoed in the air.

***Kate Fischer (13)***
***George Heriot's School***

## Christmas Dinner

Christmas is the best time of the year,
With all the presents,
And Christmas cheer,
But the bit about Christmas that I love most,
Has to be the turkey roast!

With mashed potato,
Sweetcorn and peas,
All that food,
Will make you go weak at the knees!

We have salmon and prawns,
Carrots and ham,
Cakes and gateaux,
And leg of lamb.

Well, I love the food,
I love the cheer,
Now I can't wait till it turns New Year!

***Gillian Thomson (12)***
***George Heriot's School***

## REFLECTION ON THE WORLD

Have you ever stopped to think
Why the sunset's red and pink?
Have you ever stopped and seen
An insect crawling on a bean?
Have you ever stopped to hear
The bleat of a newborn lamb that's near?
Have you *ever* stopped?

Have you ever stopped to wonder
Why there's lightning and thunder?
Have you ever stopped to touch
The leaves of a flower? Is that too much?
Have you ever stopped and thought
Why we want to know such an awful lot?
Have you *ever* stopped?

Or have you just let the world go by
And never even wondered why?

***Susan Hutchings (11)***
***George Heriot's School***

## DIANA

You had the most amazing eyes,
The most amazing smile,
Your kindness and your loving stretched for many a long mile,
The light you shone your whole life through, we cannot replace,
A life without your loving presence is so hard to face.

Now you're gone it does not seem real,
Nothing can match this pain we feel.
You shone so radiant and so bright,
So soon God extinguished your light.

Diana, we wish you were still here,
But through your sons we'll feel your love -
Now you're in heaven up above.

***Diana Tansley (14)***
***George Heriot's School***

## THE DOG

Seeing the affectionate way he gazed at me
The fiery tint of enjoyment of the sun,
Glimmering in his eyes.
Playing happily together,
Without a worry in the world,
Acknowledging only each other.
Slowly grooming his coat,
Smooth and tender like a sheet of silk.
But now you will not see that
Glimmering in his eye,
For he has no eyesight
Though that'll never come in our way
For we will always be together.

***Laurie Allan (14)***
***George Heriot's School***

## AGE

I remember seeing my granny in the old folks' home.
Seemed a waste of time, my time.
It took her a while to recognise and remember me.
Old people get like that I guess,
loss of memory, sometimes their sanity.
'Who are you,' she says.
'Granny, it's me,' I say.
'Oh yes, yes,' she replies.
I remember walking through the halls,
littered with old people; seemed like a bingo hall,
but you hear no bingo,
you hear nothing.
Nothing but the television which nobody is watching
and the gentle 'sip' of grannies and
grandads sipping their tea, coffee and the occasional
hot chocolate whilst looking into orbit.
I look at them wondering what they are thinking,
wondering if they know what is happening to them.
I think to myself they must do,
but do they when they get to that age?
I hope so.
But can you imagine yourself in their position
when you're their age
Wasting away in an old armchair,
reminiscing past times?
*I can't.*

***Cameron Drysdale (13)***
***George Heriot's School***

## Blue Plains

Dark skies drift towards the
Horizon,
Where it softly kisses the sea
Upon meeting.

The waves creep
Slowly
From the distance,
Quickening,
As its foam gallops
To the white sun-bleached sands,
Like wild horses
Dancing
On
Blue
Plains.

***Isla Leaver-Yap (14)***
***George Heriot's School***

## The Daffodil-Yellow Villa

On a hill, amongst the olive groves
Overlooking the shining sea,
The daffodil-yellow villa
Stood, midst rotting greenery.

With shutters green and roof of red,
The wilderness of flowers
Showed, spite decay and emptiness,
A sign of happier hours.

In the little sunken garden,
With the orange and lemon trees,
The orchards were still and silent
Apart from the humming of bees.

The house with its cracked and peeling walls,
Had an ancient, melancholy air,
As though the villa and landscape
Were asleep; just lying there.

***Lucy Todd (12)***
***George Heriot's School***

## GLIDING

Cable safe and secure, sir.
The wind pipes up,
You are propelled into infinity,
The adrenaline rush starts,
Getting higher and higher,
Soaring as an eagle,
Turning and winding in the currents of air,
Dropping in altitude and full of energy,
Hitting some turbulence,
Rocking in a rodeo,
Lining up the nose with the line,
Right on target,
Waiting for touch down,
Seven minutes and it feels like seconds.

***Alexander Nashed (14)***
***George Heriot's School***

## Numbed

I never thought that I could have been
so calm in a situation such as this,
My nerve cells were numbed,
The only working part of my body was the
practical part of my brain.

When my father first mentioned he thought he
was having a heart attack I dismissed it,
But as we drove through town I knew
something was wrong.
We entered the Accident and Emergency and
he was admitted almost instantly,
I had expected panic or fear but I felt nothing.

After what seemed like a lifetime, a nurse told
me we needed to get in touch with my mother.
Eventually we found her and I was left in
a small lounge by myself,
I had thought that then all these events
would sink in, but they never did.

I don't know why I didn't have the normal
reactions of my kin when this happened,
But it's over now,
And I have passed through this experience
in a peculiar way,
I feel sad that this happened but have
never panicked and never cried.

***Ryan Moffat (14)***
***George Heriot's School***

## CATS!

It was old and deserted, it was upon a hill
It was . . . the house

One evening I was playing
I thought I saw a movement in one of the windows
I dared to go close
The door creaked open
But . . . to my surprise
The house was warm and bright
And there before me was a feast
I went to eat
But suddenly the lights went out
There were green eyes all about
But what was that? There was a yowl and a creak
I felt for the door, but all I felt was an animal's coat.

I eventually get out, but the chase is on
I run and run, but they refuse to give up
I run across the bridge, I run on top of roofs
But they follow and follow
Now I am cornered
'Gimme the grub,' order the cats
'Never,' I cry
'You'll be sorry,' growl the cats
'No, I won't,' cry I
I run . . . cats flying everywhere
Like bowling pins to a ball
I run . . . still they follow
I scream, then . . . *Bump!*

I woke up . . . on the floor!
'Phew,' what was all that stuff about cats?

***Naomi Maxwell (12)***
***George Heriot's School***

## THE BATTLE OF BRITAIN

It was the big day everyone had been waiting for.
The television coverage was gaining even more.
For six whole weeks this hype had been going on,
And all of a sudden it could be gone.

Scotland and England would contest the game,
People said the result would be very close.
It was a battle Scots had been waiting for,
In the crowd people began to shed a tear.

It had been dubbed as the 'Battle of Britain',
At the end of the day one team had to win.
The suspense was terrible,
The game was unbearable.

England won the toss,
So the ref blew his whistle to start the match,
It was ever so close in the first half,
The score was 0-0 at half-time.

Going into the second half both teams were
eager to score,
All of the watching fans began to roar.
Scotland scored a marvellous try,
The crowd was on its feet.

The final minutes approached,
No one could guess what was going to happen.
The score in those minutes changed dramatically,
From 5-0 to 28-25 as a result of some
amazing play.

The final whistle blew,
Scotland had won the Cup.
The crowd was screaming with joy,
The noise was deafening.

Scotland had won a glorious match,
And Scotland had won back its pride and glory.

***Robert Stuart***
***George Heriot's School***

## It

I was alone in the dark,
Unprepared for *it!*
I was unable to comprehend *it,*
Beyond the darkest nightmares.
*It* stalked you, there was no escape,
No place to hide from *it,*
*It* would catch up, always tear
you apart.

I felt unable to trust or to try and be seen,
I tried never to leave the illusory sanctuary,
I thought I could block out the fear,
There is no sanctuary, all an illusion.
You cannot keep *it* out, however hard
you try.

*It* invades your mind, enters through any
unprotected entrance, an exposed sense.
*It* is not any single enemy, *it* can come
in many forms.

*It* is not a physical monster.

*It* is bullying!

***Jonathan Shilland (11)***
***George Heriot's School***

## The Journey

The journey ahead is long, so he sings a cheerful wee song.
He starts to go.
He creeps along past the guard, the path made for him is hard.
He's on his own.
He climbs down a large ravine, hoping he's not been seen.
His heart beats fast.
His target is miles away, how far he cannot say.
Can he get that far?
There's no point in going back, but his energy begins to lack.
He needs a rest.
The night fades into the day, his body begins to sway.
Here comes the dawn.
People are all around, he tries not to make a sound.
The search is on.
He lets loose a tear, can the end be near?
And still he runs.
On and on more, he lets out a roar.
He sees the end.
Picking up speed, with only one need.
To reach the end.
Faster he runs, nearer he comes.
He's not stopping now.
Inside the door, he's getting slower.
This is the end.
Out comes the sun, he knows he has won.
The end has come.

*Michael W Wilson (12)*
*George Heriot's School*

## A Terrible Race

I don't know when it came
I don't know where it's from
I don't know where it's going
But I do know why it's come.

It wanted a colony
On our planet Earth
Its kind had got bored
Of their land of no mirth

At first I saw one
Then I saw many
They seemed to be multiplying
And soon there were many

Once they had started
They didn't want to wait
They were not aware
Of their terrible fate

We soon realised
The humans were vanishing
We decided to stop them
We had to stop fighting

We decided to burn
The land that they lived for
And within seconds
They were all gone

Our happiness was great
We had a celebration
Little did we realise
There were two in each nation.

***Iain Hendry (11)***
***George Heriot's School***

## The Almighty Void

I looked out upon the
almighty void known as space.
The stars shone like beacons
guiding ships of space.
The vastness of the dark
still amazes me after the
many years I've served.
Some planets teemed
with life but others were
barren and lifeless.
Suddenly this deceptive
tranquillity was shattered
with a flash of the ship's
warning indicators.
The enemy had arrived
Laser beam flashes
littered the horizon
and large explosions followed.

The captain then thought
to himself: was this the
way things were to become,
an eternity of darkness
carnage and laughter amongst
the dark god.

He was awoken from his
trance with a shock, the
next wave of defenders had
come to 'play' and chaos
ruled on high once more.

***Ross Alexander (11)***
***George Heriot's School***

## THE JUNGLE

The sun slowly rises,
rays of sunshine penetrate
the canopy of treetops like lasers.
The nightlife slowly disappears
and a new day begins,
animals awaken.
Monkeys swing gracefully from
tree to tree like acrobats,
hippos rise and slowly walk
to the water like tanks
birds call out like sirens.
The hunter reveals himself from hiding,
the hunted retreat into hiding,
flying hunters swoop down
on their unsuspecting prey below,
also known as 'breakfast'!
Will the small make it through
the day without becoming a
'quick snack' for the great
hunters of the jungle?

*Yes, they do!*

The night slowly sets in and the
animals tire from the day's work.
It's all over,
or is it?

*There is still the nightlife!*

***Douglas Alexander (12)***
***George Heriot's School***

## Look

Look at the world,
A wonderful world,
Full of animals, plants and trees,
Look at a truly beautiful world.

Look at the forests,
The lakes and the mountains,
And at the hills, the trees and the rivers,
Look at a scenic, natural world.

Look at the people,
The destroyers and destructors,
Smell the pollution and see the waste,
Look at what we've done to the world.

Look at yourself,
Can you see what you're doing?
Our selfishness is taking over the Earth,
Look at the things that have disappeared.

Look at your body,
You're polluting it, as well as the land,
Why take drugs, drink alcohol or smoke?
Look at what you're doing to yourself.

Look deep down inside yourself,
Think of what our home could be like,
If everyone stopped and thought for a minute,
Look at the world, and the world that
could be.

***Fiona Wright (12)***
***George Heriot's School***

## INTENSIVE HEAT

Blades of grass quiver in a cool breeze,
Kids play together with no thought of what's
about to happen,
Mothers stop to chat with one another unaware
of the danger they're in,
Birds glide through the sky like swans in the water.

Down below under earth's crust,
A magma boils ready to rush to the surface as if
water in a tap,
A natural disaster in the form of a plague will hit
its victims in seconds,
Destroying everything in its paths.

Down in the depths of the hollowed-out pit,
The magma innocently gets ready to let its presence
be known,
It gives off little spurts as if practising for its final
great attempt,
Its energy warms up ready to burst into the fresh air.

The surface turns to a one-sided battlefield,
Natural forces overtake the power of man,
People helplessly run for their lives,
Disaster takes control without a single explanation.

***Philip Nurse (12)***
***George Heriot's School***

## Lost And Caught

I've lost my way,
I spin around,
A sudden *Crack!*
What is that sound?

Begin to run,
Cover in mind.
Something follows,
Close behind.

Running and running,
Tiring out,
Slow down slightly,
Keep looking out.

Creep into darkness,
Survey the scene,
A dark shadow moving,
I think I've been seen.

Start running again,
Till I lose my grip,
Try to get back,
Then I slip.

I stumble heavily,
Fall to the ground,
I see the light,
I know I'm found.

***Neave Corcoran (11)***
***George Heriot's School***

## Seasons Of Contrasts

Fallen leaves lie hidden under thick cold snow,
Gleaming like jewels placed on a crown of solid silver.
Colder and colder it becomes outside,
While inside I sit safely by the fire, reading,
Reading a book of enchantment and places far away,
I am in a world of contrasts.

The sky is now dark and snowflakes elegantly fall,
Like cotton wool clouds, glinting in the soft moonlight,
Slowly the silent symphony begins - snowfall,
flickering flames,
The coals in the fire glow.
Church clocks chime six o'clock in the distance,
The smell of Christmas cake wafts through the air.

Holly berries glow a deep red in a background of green,
On the bare trees a thin film of snow forms on wispy branches,
The cold, crisp air is still,
In the silence of winter the fire crackles echo,
Shadows lie on the wall, the light casting a shine like gold,
The season of contrasts has only just begun.

The clouds sail past, tinted with the lights of the moon,
Mysteriously swirling enchantingly in velvet blue sea,
Stars twinkle faintly as I watch from the window,
As clocks strike seven the fire dies down,
Snow lies on the window-pane,
The world is a mist of frosty contrasts.

***Jane Crawford (11)***
***George Heriot's School***

## FEAR

The sky is dark,
the night is here,
Something tingles inside,
A thing we call *fear!*

Your fingers go numb,
The feeling soon goes,
You shiver right from your
                    head to your toes.

Your back's dripping sweat
Your hands go clammy,
Your hair goes limp, soaking wet.

Every noise echoes,
round and round,
Your feet feel like they're *not*
touching the ground.

Your heart starts to pound,
Then misses a beat,
You feel pins and needles,
In the soles of your feet.

You hear footsteps in the hall,
In the doorway stands something tall.
The shadow seems to loom,
Then Dad enters the room.

***Rhona Grant (12)***
***George Heriot's School***

## The Fox

It was morning
The dew had fallen like diamonds on the grass
And I could feel the chill through the broken window.
I had no intention in getting up.
Had it not been for a hunger that constantly haunted my stomach.

Through the window, at the head of my bed
A movement attracted my attention
It bolted like fire along the wall
With its nose high and tail upright giving little attention to
the obstacles in its path
Its proud parade suddenly came to a hesitant halt, it paused, turned
Its head and I could see a grin of satisfaction growing on its face.

As I gaped through the window with curiosity
It dawned on me
Without a second of hesitation I flew down the stairs
I felt threatened, for the first time ever
I felt really threatened.
Charging into a stool I arrived at the wide open back door.
The tears began to roll down my cheek.
I was angry, I was afraid, I was sad.
I ran and ran and ran, screaming and yelling as I went
The devil creature stared at me casually and
Suddenly leaping, turned, tail low and sped across the wall.

My friend was safe. My only real friend.
A friend that listened.
One that always understood, a friend that loved to be cuddled
I cared little that the red beast was deprived of its meal.
It was probably sitting on someone else's rabbit hutch
Licking its chops at the expense of another poor child.
But all I cared now was that Thumper the rabbit was safe.

***Iain Murray (13)***
***George Heriot's School***

## THE DOLPHIN

The wide blue open seas stretch to all horizons,
filled with life,
as the boat shears through the waves.
The waves ride majestically,
speeding along with the boat, their speed never changing,
their white caps of foam clashing as two waves hit
in torrents of cold water.

I see a flash of blue clammy flesh,
and ignore it as a trick of the sun's reflecting on the ocean,
but again and again there is the same flash.
I rush to the bow of the boat to search for the answer,
when it is right beside me.

It is a bottle nosed dolphin,
blue with a grey underbelly and deep black eyes
as deep as the sea itself,
I stare and it stares back at me.
This highly intelligent creature is not scared of me
or the juggernaut that I travel in,
as it has probably seen many others,
some friendly, others not.

I am in awe of this beautiful creature,
I try to get closer,
I don't think,
I am not satisfied with what I have.
This may be the last chance I have to view this beast,
yet I cannot hold out to the human greed that has
destroyed so much of the Earth,
and it swims away.

That was the last I saw of a dolphin,
because of human kind's nature I have missed out.

***Mathew Smith (13)***
***George Heriot's School***

## My Fascinating Friend?

I noticed it first,
When it made friends with my fin.
I watched it, interested, but strangely scared.
And it watched me with pleasing curiosity.
Never before had I seen such a gracefully large mammal,
Almost a swimming ballerina.
And like a content ballerina would do, she danced past.
I was happy that she was satisfied, but saddened by her absence.

Later she danced for me again.
Now she had formed a fondness of me,
Or was it a grudge?
The moment her great grey bulk was directly underneath me,
So close I could see the deep blackness of her eyes,
I did not care and took the negative,
I swam, deeper
And deeper.
And when I was out of her sight,
Still swimming and panicking more viciously than I could,
I realised I was escaping to an unharmful seal.
I missed my chance
To play with her,
To swim with her,
To dance with her,
To share her gracefulness and encounter one of
The sea's greatest creatures.
How I resented what I had done,
How I'd kicked her on my pathetic departure,
And how I'd deprived myself of something few people experience.
I had missed a chance of a lifetime
To play with a seal, simply because I was scared.

***Loren Hartley (14)***
***George Heriot's School***

## A Mouse

A two-legged creature stealthily creeped upon the bush,
In which a movement was seen.

Another rustle within the bush,
Followed shortly with a dry leaf crunching on the nearby forest floor,
Made two pairs of brown eyes stop moving, stop dead in their tracks
Within the dead leaves and twigs
Of their hiding.

Soon all was silent, deadly silent,
In a moments brief pause in which all was still,
As if everything knew that two beings were waiting,
Waiting for dangers to pass.

One regarded the other with fear,
Lay stock still as the enemy approached,
As he patiently searched for this small creature,
Whose life provoked intrigue
And interest within the intruder.

The tall being watched as the rustles reappeared,
Slowly, cautiously, but as time progressed,
The brown furry creature began to emerge
From the depths of the leaves which submerged him.

And as he emerged, the observer noted
The quick, sharp eyes and the scampering feet,
Both working together to hurry away.

The lone figure left felt a strange tinge of loss,
Yet all was not lost,
For the human knew that there soon might be,
Another pause in nature,
Shared with a mouse.

***Katharine Fox (14)***
***George Heriot's School***

## THE SILENT REAPER

Bushy tail, dead give-away.
Jumps, leaps and rolls
Then still, silent
Not moving, quite stationary.
Heart stops for a second,
Seems like a year.
The squirrel.

Almost like waking up
It moves again.
Not fast, just ambling.
Without its tail
The squirrel is nothing.
A gerbil with a tail.

He's as the foot of the oak,
Its trunk of steel.
He jolts up the trunk, stopping halfway,
Observing the scene, unbelievable.
Magnets for paws, glued to the trunk,
Never falling - once again
He is moving.

The branches thin out.
The squirrel pays no extra attention,
As he leaps on twigs as fine as a hair.
He jumps, the distance seeming huge
In comparison to his tiny body.
Yet he lands
Feet poised, mind ready.
And in the flick of his tail,
He is gone.

***James Corcoran (13)***
***George Heriot's School***

## SPIDER

As I was walking through the darkened forest,
on a cold wintry morning,
with the insects buzzing in my ear as they awoke,
and the slow careful movements of a cat walking past.
I suddenly turned to see a large spider sitting
behind me on the earthy path.

Its dew dropped legs were still,
and its large black eyes were throbbing as they looked at me.

I was not scared of it, I was intrigued by it.
It looked majestic, and its beautifully coloured body
drew me towards it.

In my eyes the spider was small and vulnerable,
and as I stepped nearer to it,
the spider started to look frightened of me.

As I watched it sitting on the path,
I observed the small intricate details of its body,
and the small graceful movements which it made,
and I began to realise it felt threatened by my presence.

What should I do?
I wasn't going to let it win, but could I really kill it?

It was then I knew that I wanted to kill it,
I wanted to show that I was brave enough to do it.
The spider suddenly became big and scary,
and killing it seemed the right thing to do.
So I lifted my boot and I stamped on it.

*Dead*, it was dead.

Why had I killed it?
My conscience kept asking me, why?
I stood in disbelief, I had ended a life, so young a life,

I immediately wished I hadn't killed it.
I couldn't even bring myself to lift my boot,
I couldn't look at the remains of that spider.

I wanted it to come back,
I wanted to be able to look at it sitting on the path again,
I wished that I could see its beauty again.

***Karen Mulholland (13)***
***George Heriot's School***

## AUTUMN

The leaves fall down from the trees,
And fly away in the heavy breeze,
Red, yellow, orange and brown,
Making a carpet on the ground.

People trudge through,
Making paths which are new,
Animals prepare for the cold,
Taking as much food as they can hold.

The nights are dark,
Summer is over,
Trees are bare,
Now it is colder.

Birds fly away in flocks,
Farmers pull in their crops,
Harvest is here,
And winter is near.

***Philip Bell (12)***
***George Heriot's School***

## BATH TIME

A smell of soap filled the air,
The bath was twice as full.
I dipped my toe in carefully,
So not to burst too many.

And then I was in,
And how they covered me.
Bouncing, sailing, floating, popping,
A thick cascade of magic.

I scooped some up into my hands,
And blew them around the room.
They floated up into the air,
And suddenly they were gone.

The bath had become a volcano,
That erupted snow and cream.
A tidal wave heading straight for me,
Of cotton wool and candyfloss.

Bath time was no longer torture,
A way of causing me strife.
It was now a time for fun,
A time for smiling and for laughter.

I never wanted it to end,
I was having so much fun.
But then the plug was pulled out fast,
And my ocean flowed away.

Strangely I was not upset,
There was not a tear in my eye.
For I knew that tomorrow evening,
My kingdom of bubbles would return.

***Melanie Duncan (13)***
***George Heriot's School***

## My First Day At George Heriot's

I woke up early on the Monday morning in January.
I jumped out of bed,
And hurried to put on my new uniform.
I ate my breakfast quickly,
Then rushed through to the bathroom to brush my teeth.
I could not wait to put on the blazer.
I had never had one before.
As I was driven to school,
I counted the guest houses on the main road.
This served to calm my nerves.
It was a dark, cold and wet morning.
The large castle-like school building seemed very imposing.
As I was shown to my classroom,
I began to think about all the other schools I had been to.
I really liked the first school I had attended.
I had many friends there, the teachers were very nice.
I hated the next school.
The headmaster shouted at us in assembly,
And roared at us if we so much as coughed.
He became very angry one morning;
We all thought he was going to explode.
My third school was not much better,
But the teachers were nicer.
I was hoping this school would be like my first.
When I entered my new classroom for the first time,
I was so nervous I almost felt ill.
As the day progressed I felt less and less nervous;
I started to really like it.
Back home I could not wait to tell my mum,
And say how much I liked it,
And how like my first school it was!

***Calum Leitch (14)***
***George Heriot's School***

## A Christmas Remembered

Christmas had finally arrived.
My favourite day of the year
I had stayed up later than usual,
There was no way I could sleep.
I drifted in and out of slumber,
Checking my watch when awake.

Five o'clock in the morning
I had been sent back to bed.
Told to get up later
I had to wait some more.
I waited for what seemed like ages
Time to get up yet?
No, back to bed.

I looked out of my window
The streets were silent and dark.
The roofs of neighbouring houses
Sparkled with thin sheets of frost.
I wrote my name with my finger
In the misty patches on my window.
Each letter squeaked
As I pressed hard against the glass.

Sighing, it was back to bed,
To wait a little longer.
I must have drifted off again,
The next think I knew,
It was morning.

***Katherine Chisholm (13)***
***George Heriot's School***

## THE SORROW OF LOSING SOMETHING DEAR TO YOU

As I look into the mirror,
I see the tooth standing tall and proud
Above all the rest,
Who are sitting patiently, waiting their turn.

Swaying back and forth,
It looks so peculiar,
Compared to all the other
Sturdy, trustworthy teeth,
Who have always stood by me.

Everyday I play a tug-of-war,
Fighting the tooth to win the conflict.
All the time waiting
For the moment it will depart my mouth

Once it decides to leave,
The pain sweeps across my gum.
Then blood seeps out into my mouth.
And when I see the cause of all this pain
Sitting in my hand
I want to cry.

I want my tooth to go back,
I don't like the empty gap
Between two other tall ivory towers,
It's like a hole in my life.

I feel like I've lost a big part of me,
I won't be the same without it.
But when I see the new tooth
Protruding up to rise among the towers,
I realise that life won't be completely ruined,
A new one is just beginning.

***Kirsty McFarlane (14)***
***George Heriot's School***

## WHEN DAD DROPPED BOB DOWN THE TOILET

I watched in fascination as Bob reached the surface.
His tank was murky and green
And had a putrefied stench.
He faced me
As his mouth moved like his name,
'Bob, Bob, Bob.'
I knew he was distressed,
I could almost hear him calling out,
'Bob's tank needs cleaning!'

Dad carried Bob's small tank into the bathroom.
Like any three year old child
To me an event like this was exciting -
Bob's tank was going to be cleaned.
I held my breath as the repulsive tank neared me.
Bob began to manoeuvre to and fro quickly,
I knew he was scared and unsure.
Dad began to tip some of the tank water down the toilet.
It all seemed to happen so quickly.

The water gushed out,
It was powerful like a waterfall.
Bob took one last look at me,
I took one last look at Bob.
Time went slowly,
Bob just went with the flow.
There was an almighty crash,
The tank shattered.
Bob was gone.

'Dad,' I howled.
Tears ran down my face.
The glass was cleared up . . .
The toilet was flushed.

***Jodie Oliver (14)***
***George Heriot's School***

## THE THING THAT GOES BUMP IN THE NIGHT

I was lying innocently in my bed,
When I felt something scuttle up my leg,
I bravely turned my head,
And there it was, perched upon my knee.

Its hairy, black body was of a colossal size,
With eight, long, scaly, black legs,
Supporting its hideous body.

The giant, beady, blood red eyes,
Were glowing like beacons in the night sky,
They were full of evil and wickedness,
Just sitting there glaring straight at me.

It started to edge further up my leg.
So I picked up the nearest book,
And slammed it down upon its head.
I shuddered as I felt the crunch of its bones,
Against the softness of my leg.

The guilt overwhelmed me,
As I saw its grisly corpse embedded in my book,
I flung it across the room.
Then returned to the peaceful harmony of my bed.

Thoughts were rushing through my head,
'I was a murderer, I'd just destroyed someone's life.'
But I was also overcome with relief,
As I realised it would not come any further up my leg.

***Bryony Wade (13)***
***George Heriot's School***

## The Bike Ride

The bike wobbled from side to side.
I clenched the unfamiliar handlebars.
My hands were shaking.
I heard the encouraging voice of my dad,
As he held the back of the seat.
I began to relax.
The sweat built up on my face.
My dad assured me I could cycle.
I was determined to succeed.
Together we progressed forward,
Slow and steady.
My dad was pushing me onwards,
Supporting my bike.
I lost my balance,
But we started again.
Once again I stumbled.
I lowered my head,
Like a soldier defeated at battle.
I looked up to my dad,
He still smiled.
Detecting my impatience,
He convinced me I was improving.
It was an uphill struggle,
But I had almost reached the top.
He was constantly boosting my confidence.
We began to pick up speed.
I felt much more positive.
My dad let go of the bike.
I kept going.
He cried with joy.
I echoed.

*Catriona Johnstone (14)*
*George Heriot's School*

## Does Nobody Care?

Why I remember this so vividly I will never know,
It seems like a symbol of the holidays in my childhood.
The rain poured down on the windows and I traced it with my finger.
My parents talked of things I never understood,
And my brother teased me non-stop.
I wondered when we would be there but daren't ask again.
Again I turned to watch the sheets of rain coating the fields.
The car came to a halt and we had reached our destination.
We met up with our friends and they all chatted happily.
They located our holiday home and walked in.
I struggled up the massive stone steps,
They were sharp and menacing compared to my height.
Why can they all manage them fine?

The next day rain poured down again, I wanted to play outside,
I busied myself with dolls and I felt left out once again.
The rain began to cease and I felt instantly better,
'It'll be slippery' I heard mum say in the distance.
I wanted to play tig but I was outvoted and we played hide.

I saw the large sharp steps and headed towards them,
I was trying to trick my older brother and find somewhere sneaky.
Quickly I clambered down and felt my heart race,
I screamed as I tumbled down the menacing stairs.
Blood gushed from my leg and everyone carried on playing.
Mum ran to me and ordered everyone in.
'We've done nothing wrong' they chorused,
'Why do we have to suffer because of her?'
I buried my face in my mum's jumper and cried,
'Does nobody care?'

***Lynne Williamson (14)***
***George Heriot's School***

## SPIDER

We sat staring at the sky,
There were no stars, it was too cloudy.
Snuggled up in cocoons of linen,
The bedside lamp flickered with light and radiated with heat.

As we talked and laughed together merrily,
The room was still and silent.
It was getting late,
We were about to slip away into a deep dark sleep,

When, just for a second,
A sudden movement caught my eye,
With the swiftness of an arrow and the silence of a mouse,
A spider bolted up the wall.

In a flash my companion was across the other side of the room,
He shouted 'Kill it! Kill it!'
But no, not me, I couldn't,
What had he ever done to me? I pondered.
I tried to catch him.
He darted away. Gone.

The room fell silent, I could hear the wind gusting,
Where had he gone?
I saw him leave the room, so followed,
There I caught him and within a couple of seconds
he was out the window.

My friend cheered but for a second I felt guilt:
Was he OK? Had he landed safely?
I could only hope.
I settled down and fell asleep with a strange
reassurance that he was fine.
Then I dreamt.

***Scott MacKay (13)***
***George Heriot's School***

## THE RACE

As the moon surged into the open
She cast her ghostly beams o'er the Earth.
She coated it in silky white,
Slowly emitting her dim light.
With each movement, the stars were enchanted
And proudly they cheered her on.
She raced elegantly through the sky,
Leaving the vast dark emptiness behind her.

Suddenly the sun appeared, still weak from his long rest
But quickly gathering strength.
His pace quickened until he caught her
And they raced along, side by side.
As the sun began to radiate his warmth,
The moon's strength waned and she cried in pain.
But there was no time for mercy,
As the bitter race went on.

The morn had almost begun and
The bird-song signalled the end was near.
The moon, now tired and spent, struggled on
Until it was all over
When, alas, the sun overtook her.
She had done her best, but her time was over.
Slowly she faded away in the distance
For now, the new day had begun.

***Christopher Medley (13)***
***George Heriot's School***

## CIRCLES

The sun creeps through the curtains
Chasing away all the horrors of the night.
The monsters that plague
Children's dreams
Disappear.
Like the perfume of a flower
In the wind.
Only a trace is left
Embedded in the mind
To be revived,
When darkness rears its head
And swallows the comfort of the day.

Through the frosted glass
A bird cries for its mother.
It demands food,
To feed its never ending hunger.
The mother, already tired,
Takes its every desire
Like a command.

The first of the morning traffic
Is a gentle hum in the background,
And the world begins to fill up once more.
Endless streams of people rushing
To places, never stopping
To think.
Like rats on a wheel,
Going round
And round
In circles.

***Louisa Young (14)***
***George Heriot's School***

## My Great Day

I crawled out of bed an hour late
With no time for piping hot water,
Lavished generously over my face.
No time for make-up application,
Only enough time for
Being catapulted into my uniform;
And looking forward to my great day.

A sprint start out the door,
Sent me flying round the corner.
Losing control I collapsed in a heap,
With papers flying,
Crumpled uniform,
And baggy eyes that should be hidden
Under a thick layer of
Compact powder and foundation.

I picked myself up and dusted down.
Looking up I caught sight of the bus,
Cursing and swearing, I flew towards it.
When the bus driver saw me,
He then decided to drive off.
After watching the big red car pull away,
I gave up, nothing was going right,
On that great day of mine.

***Funmi Oyeneyin (14)***
***George Heriot's School***

## THE HOSPITAL

The oppressive atmosphere, warm and stuffy,
The lonely corridor,
Silent except for the muffled padding of rubber soled shoes.
The sterile walls of white and lingering smell
Of disinfectant invading every crevice.
The colourful paintings, vivid streaks,
Trying, unsuccessfully, to enliven disheartened souls.

The ill patients, slowly trundling along with
Drawn and taut features, stare blankly along endless corridors.
A sudden 'thump', awakens me from a trance like state,
And as I cast a fluttering glance,
In an attempt of an apology,
My look is sharpened, into a morbid, and fascinated stare.

Her face is streaked with irreversible horror,
Her cheeks scarred with pain,
The swelling of the scalding, hot, accident
Not yet gone.
Her face is etched with the hurtful memory,
A physical reminder, always there,
The burns' victim looks helplessly at me,
Pleading for an escape from her pain.

I can't help staring, yet I know I must look away to be inconspicuous,
Disgusted at myself and ashamed, for staring,
The permanent marks, forever with her,
Reflect the frightening reality of her wounds.

The question of who? What? Where? Why?
Run round in my mind like a train on a never ending track.
She has now realised that I am staring,
And so, both turning red-faced, continue walking,
My embarrassment for being caught,
And hers for being in the wrong place at the wrong time.

***Ashlie-Jayne Allcock (14)***
***George Heriot's School***

## Oblivion

Eternal darkness.
No light enters -
No light even exists.
The endless void.

The stars are lost for all time,
The continual battle of
*Dark* and *Light*
Has been fought and lost.
All existence is but
Darkness.

The illusion of light,
Dispelled once and for all.
No shadow,
No gloom.
Nothing beyond the dark.

Much as we may want
All there can be is darkness.
And so,
We enter
*Oblivion!*

***Finlay Young (12)***
***George Heriot's School***

## TEACHERS

As you come into the classroom they stare at you,
With their evil eyes.
They follow you to your seat,
And start to hypnotise.

You sit down,
Into a false sense of security.
They give you a vocabulary test,
And you are asked to spell 'ingenuity'.

And of course you spell it wrongly,
But as you await your doom.
Out of the blue they say,
'Never mind, you'll be able to spell it soon.'

I guess you can
Never tell with teachers.
Especially if they teach
English!

***Paul Masterton (11)***
***George Watson's College***

## INFINITY, INFINITY, INFINITY

I mpossible to count to
N ever starting, never finishing
F orever lasting
I nfinity is incomparable
N othing can compete
I nvisible to every eye, it is without limits
T hough we will never last that long, the
Y ears count its endless life.

***Euan McGhee (12)***
***George Watson's College***

## EXAM FEVER

The hall falls silent,
pens begin to scrawl,
and scribble,
and scrape.
I glance over
first right,
then left.
What are they writing?
How can they know so much?
I search my mind -
the answers must be there,
somewhere?
I stare down at my paper,
words swim,
then start to run away.
Breathe deeply.
Breathe deeply.
Just read,
think,
write.
If only it was that simple!
I drop my pen in despair.
I jump up and turn to go,
faces look and eyes stare.
If only I knew what they know.

***Sophie Patterson***
***George Watson's College***

## WAR

Here I am
In the middle
Of war
Two sides both determined
To win
It's not fair
Why do we
Have to be
Stuck in the middle?
Why don't they
Leave us alone?
When I'm older
I'll make
World peace
Until then
I'll keep
Waiting
Wishing
Hoping
That it will end soon.

***Euan Granger (12)***
***George Watson's College***

## SNOW

Sheets of glistening white,
Stretching for miles,
Covering the world.

Drifts so deeply soft,
Like piles of chalk dust,
Fallen from the sky.

Wisps of green push through,
From below layers of white,
Now patchy and crunchy.

Beautiful scenes fade away,
As what was once lovely,
Is now a slushy grey mess.

***Lindsay Robertson (12)***
***George Watson's College***

## The Bird

It flew higher and higher,
Up and up into the night,
Reaching high above others,
In a solitary flight.
Speedily soaring through the air,
Achieving a really great height.
Wing span over a meter long,
Elegance shining like a light.

Now, with head lowered down,
It startled the prey below.
Through the eyes of the lone hunter,
It sought the prey it stole.
Suddenly sensing the hunter's presence,
The prey darted into a hole.
Dismayed at the sudden prospect,
The bird got away without its goal.

***Yuan Shen (11)***
***George Watson's College***

## THROUGH A CAT'S EYES

There he is, quick as a flash,
Running across the grass.
Here he comes back again,
Will it ever end?

Soon enough, it will come to an end
When I pounce on him.
Slowly does it,
He doesn't know I'm here.
Quietly creep up on him
So he doesn't know.
One, two, three,
Pounce!

Where's he gone?
He was just here,
Right beside me,
On the grass.
Where can he be?

There he is under the tree,
I'll have better luck this time.
I'm going to get that mouse!

***Rosemary Turnbull (12)***
***George Watson's College***

## FEAR

We all harbour fears,
we may not know why.
Some may last years,
or the blink of an eye.
No matter your colour, race or creed,
maybe fear's something all of us need.

We may fear the future
and what it may hold
if we shall crumble
or stay proud and bold!
Bad things will happen
how will we cope?
to cancel out fear we must also have hope.

*Clive Ferenbach (16)*
*George Watson's College*

## Just Maybe

You should always speak your mind,
Don't keep things
Bottled up.
If you want to say something,
Then say it.
Feel free, do as you please.
Don't follow others,
Follow your heart.
Answer back, get your message across.
Be understood.
You are unique. Stay that way.
Always do what you feel is right.
Don't keep things bottled up.

Maybe if I had listened to all this,
Maybe if I had listened,
Maybe,
Maybe.

Just maybe.

*Lucy Berkengoff (12)*
*George Watson's College*

## THE KNIFE

The silver blade glints menacingly.
The smooth, sly handle feels comfortable in my hand.
I roll it around,
Stroking and caressing it with my thumb.
My distorted reflection
Glares back at me with glazed-over eyes.
I run my index finger over the serrated edge
And pull back in pain when it nicks me.

I plunge the point into its victim,
And drag the knife slowly down;
It pleases me to feel the slicing sensation.
As I pull the blade out,
I can sense the slurping resistance.
I almost feel sympathy towards the poor orange.

***Melanie Belford (15)***
***George Watson's College***

## TRAINS

When Railtrack,
Kept turning trains back,
They never got out of the station,
The points got bashed,
The trains all crashed,
It was now the fear of the nation!
Directors talked,
People now walked,
And drivers found a new occupation.

***Philip McKinnon (11)***
***George Watson's College***

## Devastation

Look around you
What do you see?
Is it a place fit for you and me?

Go outside. Breathe the air.
What have we done to our planet?
Is it fair?

On our doorstep a global disaster,
Kill a rainforest a minute?
No - even faster.

The sea is our friend. The fish and whales our cousins.
We pollute it no end,
But still it recovers.

Nuclear wars for no good reason,
Winning not losing,
Always seems to please them.

But what if we're losing
A battle against the elements.
The sun and the rain. No ozone layer to save us.

We're losing a battle for our only home,
There's no way to stop it,
Our planet from pain it groans.

The greenhouse effect - our very own doing,
Now life ain't so good,
In fact it's quite gloomy.

It could all be different,
If we stop pollution right now,
No cars, no fumes,
But we don't want to know how.

***Morag Macniven (12)***
***George Watson's College***

## Childhood

When under the protection of childhood
We are young, and wish to break free
From the barrier that holds us.
We seek respect,
And rebel against authority.
The warm, comforting cover of childhood
Seems so immense if trapped in it.
We wait impatiently
For the slow ride through dependence to end.
Desperately seeking
The adulthood just out of view.

When this goal is finally reached
And the protection is taken away,
We are vulnerable and open.
Without the bliss of ignorance and innocence to protect us
Hunting for other things to hide behind
Thinking that we have missed out
On the best years of our lives.

***Sam Medrington (16)***
***George Watson's College***

## Recurring Memories

I try not to reflect,
But the past persists.
It parades itself through my head.
Like unended images screaming to a point.
Mirrors reflect my gregarious history
Repeating, repeating, repeating itself.
Why him, why me, . . . why?

We blaze with angel-like eternity,
Embracing our star.
Through the translucent universe
But the breaking mechanism of the past
Drags us to an unending fall.
Why him, why me?
Why anyone?

***Victoria Wason (16)***
***George Watson's College***

## THE HOWLING WIND

The wind howls through the hedgerows,
Sending leaves flying.
It goes roaring round trees,
Making them shiver.
It roars and howls through the forest,
Making a racket.

The wind goes growling down the chimney,
Making the chimney wobble.
It goes pounding against the walls,
Making the brickwork rattle.
It roars through the slack tiles,
So that they rattle against the roof.
The gale force wind makes the whole house shake!

The wind goes roaring over the ocean,
Making the waves lash against each other.
It goes crashing against the rocks,
Sending spray flying.
It goes pounding up the beach,
Making the waves go screeching over the sand.

***Ruth Leslie Gibson (12)***
***George Watson's College***

## A Sonnet

You stand, you look at the world at your feet
Through eyes that are blue but only see gold
Your heart is frozen, your laugh with no heat
You think warmth and compassion, to me you are cold
You say you're a man but you're really a boy
In manners you're blessed with little or none
Playing my feelings as you would with a toy
You shoot me with words, your lips like a gun
Inside you there's something which draws me in
These feelings I hold which I cannot shed
I know it's right but it feels like sin
Saying you love me words float through my head
We, like love and light stand bright together
With you I feel love will last forever.

***Anya Barry (16)***
***George Watson's College***

## Volcano!

A rumbling sound, deep in the earth,
A great bang, painful to my ears.
Thundering, crashing, the explosion awaits,
Ready to murder and deafen.
The volcano erupts, scaring the land,
Smoke bursting out, turning day into night.
Flames shooting everywhere.
Oranges, yellows and reds light the dark sky,
A river of lava flows down the mountainside.
Children cry for their mothers.
Mothers scream for their children.
Then, there is complete silence.

***Gillian Myles (12)***
***George Watson's College***

## OUR PLANET

Look what we're doing,
Does anyone stop to?
Surely if we were put on the earth,
We were meant to look after it.

Look what we're doing,
Does anyone stop to?
If God intended us to have pollution-mobiles,
He would have had them at the start.

Look what we're doing,
Does anyone stop to?
Global warming and the ozone layer,
Everyday words to most of us.

Look what we're doing,
Does anyone stop to?
Natural resources used up all too soon,
Who's the next person you're going to blame?

Look what we're doing,
Does anyone stop to?
Acid raining down on us every day
Always someone else's fault.

But it's not someone else's fault,
It's your world as well . . .

***Eilidh Macdonald (13)***
***George Watson's College***

## The Monster

He went to the park at night,
Not really expecting a fright.
But if he knew what was coming his way,
He would have only gone during the day.

When he walked along,
He was singing a song.
But there was a voice in his head,
He was told to go back or be dead.

He went along anyway,
But now he doesn't have much to say.
He saw it coming far too late,
But it had decided his fate.

He was having fun,
When his friend turned to run.
It was then his friends fled,
Leaving him for dead.

He turned around and tried to scream,
When his eyes started to gleam.
When he tried to run away,
He fell down and to his dismay,

It was on him like a shark,
But worse of all was his fearsome bark.
It hit his head on the ground,
And gobbled him up without a sound.

So remember what I say,
And listen to your head today.
Or you might end up just like him,
With your soul growing dim.

***Paul Fleming (12)***
***George Watson's College***

## BRACE

On Friday I got a brace
Around my teeth like a lace,
I walked out of the dentists' surgery, happy enough,
Then suddenly,
'Ouch, ouch, ouch!'

On my brace, there's a wire
That burns like a fire,
Like a fire,
Burning into my gums.
'Ouch, ouch, ouch!'

I went back to my house,
Where, in pain, I squeaked like a mouse.
I was screaming in agony,
'I want rid of this thing!
Ouch, ouch, ouch!'

To my mum I went and said:
'I want to go to bed.'
So up I went,
And had a rest.
'Ouch, ouch, ouch!'

There was lots of pain,
And to sleep, was an awful strain.
But despite all this, I had forty winks,
But suddenly
'Ouch, ouch, ouch!'

I went to the dental hospital,
And a dentist looked at it all.
She fixed me up, I was just fine,
But suddenly
'Ouch, ouch, ouch!'

***Jamie Sutherland (12)***
***George Watson's College***

## THE SEA

Under the sea is a beautiful place,
There are lovely plants and lots of space,
The animals there can live in peace,
But now that life is bound to cease.

Now man has come and seen it all,
And soon we'll have to watch it fall,
What we had before, an unharmed ocean,
Is now suffering from our pollution.

But still there is some time to mend,
And still there is time to defend,
The beautiful animals under these seas,
So help them, help them, help them please.

***Negin Ghorbani Moghaddam (12)***
***George Watson's College***

## THE HOLD

All your life you tried to escape
And now you have and what's the point?
Now you're free and your life can take shape
And now you can and what's the point?

Your whole life on the run
Your whole life running to this
And now finally it's begun
But you can't see the point anymore.

You spat on the grave and swore he was dead
But now you see he's still alive
But now he's alive, living in your head
And the hold's still there, forever with you.

***Laura Crombie (14)***
***George Watson's College***

## THE COLOUR YELLOW

As I lie on my back,
in the French summer,
the dust I kick
up floats slowly into the air,
supplying it with a sophisticated
sense of
mass.
The strong afternoon sunlight,
filtering
        through
                the umbrella
                        of trees,
furnishes the atmosphere
with a yellow quality,
like the sunflowers that prosper
in the fields around.

As I lounge by the telly,
in the Scottish winter,
the rain clouds throw
down falls through the air,
imposing upon it
a feeling of
mass.
The weak mid-winter sunlight
and; the flickering; street;
        lamp; outside;
                reflecting in; the puddles;
                        on; the paving stones,
forces upon the atmosphere
a yellow property,
like the dandelions that prosper
in the cracks in the pavement.

***Richard Struthers (16)***
***George Watson's College***

## My Cat

Oh my fat, beautiful cat,
How loveable you look today,
All snug and warm,
In that odd cosy form,
Sprawled out in that cute, careless way.

Your eyes are shut tight,
To keep out the light,
Of the shining picture,
From the TV so bright.

And although there is noise,
Your mind is asleep,
While you lie there contentedly,
In a doze so very deep.

Your nose is well hidden,
Beneath a tail so fat,
Because that round ball of fluff,
Is supposed to be my cat.

I love you Alfie,
My dear old friend,
And I will always love you,
Until the end.

***Louise Auld-Smith (12)***
***George Watson's College***

## Sherkin Island

A lonely boat sits peacefully in the Horseshoe Bay
unaware of the rest of the world.
The crystal water swirls gently with the icy morning breeze.
The waves flowing slowly and smoothly over rocks like
a crystal blanket.

As we walk the long path, we look out to see emptiness,
the sky like a blank canvas.
The island, still unspoilt by city life, pollution noise
The soaring hills enclose this isolated world.
A loud blast from a passing cargo ship reminds us
of the bustling city and the real world.

The illusion is gone . . .

***Charlotte Faichney (13)***
***George Watson's College***

## THE SEABED

What endless wonders,
Does the sea behold?
A fish's realm,
Untouched and undiscovered,
Beneath the rolling waves.

Maybe there lives a giant creature,
With huge chomping teeth.
Or maybe just a minnow,
Small and helpless,
In a vast and empty ocean.

Like a desert on land,
The sand lies smooth and bare.
With its own mountains and cities,
Of pretty coral and weeds,
Which lie untouched,
On the ocean bed.

***Ally Dick (13)***
***George Watson's College***

## A Watch

I look down at you,
To tell me the time,
And say it's alright,
And everything's fine.

The soft feel of the strap,
Makes my wrist feel complete,
You are so small and soft,
But comfortable and neat.

Without you my wrist,
Can feel so bare,
Without you I'm helpless,
And full of despair.

I look down at you,
To see everything's well,
When I'm sitting in lessons,
That bore me like hell!

***Andrew Waters (16)***
***George Watson's College***

## A Bed

Plain and simple
Soft and comforting
A place of warmth and homeliness

Reminder to a window,
Like heaven for lovers.

Escape for some,
Yet, for many still a 'dream'.

***Douglas Garner (16)***
***George Watson's College***

## The Caribbean Dream

The water is pure and crystal-like
Being gently shaken by the rare fluffy clouds
Swiftly moving east
Leaving this paradise island.

I step out from my perfect beach house
Into the glistening light
I breathe and take in all the wonderful smells
And the exotic landscape,
And run down the magnificent white sand
To a familiar cliff.

I look over the drop,
Excellent!
I slowly walk backwards,
Then run with all my might and jump!
Falling, falling
Into the wonders of the luscious coral reefs and the
Untouched sea.
I squeal with pure delight and *splash!*
Into the water I go.
I come to the shaking surface and laugh.

Kitty, Kitty!
I hear a voice, calling my name.
Wake up, you're late for school
No, no! It was all a dream!
Everything! Gone in a flash!
I lie down miserably and go back to sleep.

***Kitty Colquhoun (12)***
***George Watson's College***

## My Perfect Image

Their vibrant colour so wild, so free,
so many shades of dancing gold.
Slightly stirring in the passing breeze,
Warm, soft, sweet, delicate.

We do not have time to take in everything,
but the sunflowers notice.
They seem to be watching you,
like the internal eye of a painting.

They glow with a magical radiance,
like the newly washed face of a youngster.
But some look so old, so withered.
My perfect image is spoiled.

In the end they shall wilt away,
like the hope of a hostage.
Leaving only a vague scent,
on the canvas of my mind.
My perfect image shall be no more.

***Lisa Hunter (14)***
***George Watson's College***

## The Silence Is Broken

In the dead of the night,
The silence is broken.
It breaks with a shuddering, shattering bang,
It's started again the little ones said.

The houses smash,
The people scream;
The bombs are relentless,
Like the flow of a stream.

Why must they fight,
Why must we be labelled,
Will it ever end?
Ask the men round the tables.

***Chris Sinclair (16)***
***George Watson's College***

## IMAGES

Relaxing in the cool, calm breeze,
Birds singing as if there was a choir in the sky,
A mystical, magical world.

An everlasting view, with hills as tall as the never ending sky,
The towering tree is the sole protector of the ice cold lake,
Admiring himself in it he stares, mesmerised into the deep depths
Reaching out to find the secrets held within the lake's precious skin,
Like a person reaching for their inner soul..

The rain moisturises the house's rough skin,
The air devouring the house's decaying walls,
Is dark, dank, dreary.

Sweet, honey, smelling grass,
Animals scurrying, playfully about in the bushes,
Shadows playing tricks on your mind.

The wild wind's long, boney fingers,
Wrap around you like
A witch cradling her cunning, conniving cat.

The elusive house alone,
Nestling behind the bristling bush,
Hiding all its long held mysteries.

***Kirsty Macpherson (14)***
***George Watson's College***

## FEAR: THE TERRORIST

The man who takes the blame,
Yet he can't feel the pain,
Husbands, daughters, sons and wives,
What is the value of human lives?

To lay a package in a hollow space,
He does not see the death with his face,
A callous, inhuman, act of man,
He represents his country the only way he can.

Devastation and destruction,
He views the aftermath of the eruption,
Debris lying on the road,
Of the government that his bombs goad.

***Simon Beggs (16)***
***George Watson's College***

## MORNING

In the morning the early bird sings
He clears his throat and stretches the wings

He catches a worm that squirms and squiggles
As it's carried away, it wriggles and wriggles

The cat next door prowls around
The breeze in the trees is the only sound

He starts to search for his daily mouse
So he can take it back to his cosy house

The morning is the start of a new day
With all the wildlife coming out to play.

***Laura Ross (13)***
***George Watson's College***

## RAPID LIFE

All is quiet, yet gradually
A noise can be heard in the distance,
A noise like the sound of the sea through a shell
Louder and louder, stronger and stronger.

As we approach the white water-like foam
Bubbling and swirling with a mind of its own,
The waves curl like giant fingers
And slice in half when they hit the rocks.

By now, the noise so loud is threatening and fierce.
The waves take me up and down like a roller-coaster.
The water splashing in my face, blinding me,
Yet still, I carry on.

The water swirls in little whirlpools, inviting any passers-by.
The waves like people fighting against each other, roar like thunder.
The wind blows in my face as I pull my paddle through the water.
Yet still, I carry on.

At last, the water is calming, the tension is dropping.
Only small ripples and cracks can be seen on the water.
Soon, the water releases all its strength and regains its stillness,
And once again, all is quiet.

***Heather Jackson (13)***
***George Watson's College***

## Starry Night

Why is the world such a mean place?
War, poverty, death.
You sit wondering what will
happen next, an earthquake,
a bomb scare, a shooting?

The wind is mean enraged by the world
an image of me when I understand
what's going on.
The stars are shining telling us the news
but we don't listen, we don't want to know.

The sky is our commander
looking down on us,
a small innocent town
our world is ruined.
All that remains is the powerful sky.

Our sky hidden by the stars.
Overcrowded, overpowered.
Our insignificant town hidden by the sky.
Together they make,
Our world.

***Jennifer C Macleod (13)***
***George Watson's College***

## THE 'LOST' CHILD

I was a 'lost' child.
Forever escaping the bind of my mother's hand.
Meditating as I stroll along the high street,
I smile to myself,
As grown ups can when reflecting on their infancy.
At first I enjoyed the freedom;
I was a brave little explorer in a land of giants.
But soon I would become frightened,
Lost in a world over whose entrance was written
'Supermarket', in neon lights,
Stranded between mountains of baked bean tins
And seas of fresh bread and rolls,
Dodging to avoid the grey caged monsters, with
Squeaking wheels, which bore down on me.
Then I would cry,
And always, out of nowhere, my mother would appear,
To reassure me in her arms,
A familiar face, safe and secure.

I stop,
Have been walking for hours.
The air is cool and sky darkening.
The street unfamiliar, passers-by hostile,
And I am surrounded by tenement buildings,
Beside which I am an ant.
Suddenly, I am a lost child again.

***Laura Robertson (16)***
***George Watson's College***

## A DOUBLE-SIDED LIFE

Some people are blind,
As they wander through life.
Taking for granted what they have,
Ignorant of the pain and strife.
Of the third world people, so brave.

People such as these don't choose to suffer,
Despite what others think.
Every day is a struggle to survive,
To them it's swim or sink.

Yet it is these who don't want charity,
Just help to become independent.
To these people,
Proper work for men,
Would score a perfect ten.

Others who take their possessions for granted,
May not choose to be so dismissive,
But for some people, as they say,
'Ignorance is bliss.'

***Katie Skellett (13)***
***George Watson's College***

## REGRET

A quiet little scream,
inside my mind.
A clever little punch,
in my ribs.

The reoccurring nightmare,
that keeps me awake.
The constant reminders,
that lurk at every step.

That feeling of regret,
takes time to go away.
It will haunt me until
I can't remember what went wrong.

***Beth McKeown (16)***
***George Watson's College***

## DUST

A soul of lost memories,
covering forgotten things.
A gentle film over objects,
abandoned by humour,
Easing their pain.

Clinging to broken light bulbs,
as the moths once did before.
Dulling a mirror's surfacing,
calming its angry glare
In anticipation.

The ancient chest lies,
as if in lonely exile.
Tiny spirits coating their thoughts,
old letters, fading pictures,
Very much alive.

In a dreary attic
a grandmother's thoughts.
Now a loving, silvery notion,
hugging, not abandoning,
The abandoned.

***Michael Rainey (13)***
***George Watson's College***

## SOLDIER

Soldier, soldier, fighting, dying,
For a country well beloved,
Wife and children, weeping, crying,
For a good man they still love.

For his country, for his flag,
For its empire, for its wealth,
He goes home in a black bag,
No one cared much for his health.

A life in a slum, a death in a field,
All for his 'mother' in her glory,
For all her wealth he scarcely mealed,
No one though to tell the story.

America, Australia on the world's other side,
Africa, India, diamonds and gold,
For all these he fought and died,
Ever serving, ever bold.

At least he died for his country, they say,
At least he died in war,
But his sons still work in the great coal mines,
Doesn't he deserve more?

***Joshua Abramsky (12)***
***George Watson's College***

## GOLDEN STAR

Golden star
Shining bright
Like a candle
In the night

Golden star
Twinkle on
In the dark
Never gone.

***Sarah Yellowlees (13)***
***George Watson's College***

## INDECISION

Will I? Won't I?
Should he? Shouldn't he?
Do they? Don't they?
Could she? Couldn't she?

So much time is spent,
(But is that time well spent?)
To wonder and to ponder,
Over which, what and why?

How mistaken would the world be
To make the choice, yes or no,
On the spot,
I just don't know!

Do the fools not have it
Or am I the fool to endure it?
Because the fool who has it may make the right choice,
But he who does not may have the carefree day.

So much indecision,
We all have inside,
Is the worry worth it?
This I can't decide!

***Donna Bryce (13)***
***George Watson's College***

## Only a Game?

They turn out in their thousands every week,
From every walk of life, from every street.
Merged into one Bovril slurping, pie munching atmospheric cauldron,
And in the middle of it all, are two teams and a ball.

Supporters with their dogmatic, biased views about their team,
All with their need for goals, their hopes and dreams.
Merged into one nail-biting, finger crossing atmospheric cauldron,
And in the middle of it all, are two teams and a ball.

The players on the field just get on with it,
All with determined, focused, sheer grit.
Merged into one perspiring, aggressive atmospheric cauldron,
And in the middle of it all, are two teams and a ball.

The commercial game they call the big scene,
Can't be recreated by flashing pictures on a screen.
Merged into one money spinning, profit making atmospheric cauldron,
And in the middle of it all, are two teams and a ball.

Bill Shankly you should bow your head in shame,
It's really only just a game.
Merged into one single-minded, truly obsessive atmospheric cauldron,
And in the middle of it all, are two teams and a ball.

The stage is set, the whistle sounds.
There's only once place, the football ground.

***Craig MacNee (12)***
***George Watson's College***

## The Spirit Of Winter

October days are getting colder,
And winter traditions getting older

Old Jack Frost is almost here,
The snowy winter is very near

Snowballs, snowmen short and tall,
Sledging is fast and most fun of all

Christmas carols being sung,
To entertain both old and young

On Christmas day we give and share,
And get together to show we care

But of these things what's best for me,
Is spending time with my family.

*Danielle Kennedy (12)*
***Inveralmond Community High School***

## Monsters In My Room

M ysterious monsters under my bed.
O h no not another sleepless night.
N oisy monsters chewing my slippers.
S cary shadows on my wall.
T error, horror about a hundred in all.
E volution when they tuck into my homework jotter like scavengers.
R uthless and heartless could care for no one.
S miles in the morning when it was all just a dream.

*Louise Storrar (12)*
***Inveralmond Community High School***

## Night And Day!

The sun shines up in the bright blue sky
It is round like the shape of a big apple pie

It hides behind clouds that are fluffy and white
And goes away when the day turns to night

At night when it's dark the full moon comes out
And you can see it when you're out and about

But I prefer for it to be day
So I can go up to the park and play

At night when it's dark, I go to my bed
But bang goes the door on the garden shed

I lie in my bed and look up and pray
That this cold, dark night will soon turn to day.

***Donna Smith (12)***
***Inveralmond Community High School***

## An Orthodox Visitor

An orthodox visitor, as anyone would say,
had distinguished features, which a person could gaze
upon a mile away.

The miniature eyes hung above his face, walking on his
seven toed feet at a steady pace.

His scarlet fur stuck out, slime dripped off his nose.
He could not speak or wink an eye. All he could do was
mime his scary greeting.

***Christopher Jeffery (12)***
***Inveralmond Community High School***

## FEELINGS

You're in a dark forest surrounded by weak trees, you're lonely,
you hear footsteps in amongst the leaves, you're frightened,
you turn round quickly on one foot, you're shaking,
it's foggy, wind brushes against your face, a shiver goes down
your spine.
The drifting fog turns into thunder and lightning, I am cold and wet,
my clothes are damp, my skin is frozen, what should I do?
I hide under a tree behind a branch, from the noises,
from the fog, from the wind, from the deadly rain, I stop to shiver.
The rain has stopped, the wind and the fog eases its way away,
I am no longer frightened, the dark gloomy light turns to day.

***Jennifer Connelly (11)***
***Inveralmond Community High School***

## THE SCHOOL

Inveralmond is the school
Where no bullying is the rule
In geography you learn a lot
In English you read in a room that's hot.
In maths you learn, where to put the dot
In history how the Romans fought.
In art you learn to draw the line
In CDT you work in time.
The other subjects are all fine
But in the end the main rule is
No bullying.

***Susan McKnight (11)***
***Inveralmond Community High School***

## GRANDAD

The rain was falling hard
as hard as one million basketballs bouncing
everyone was quiet, but the vicar
he was reading the Lord's Prayer
my mum and sister are crying
I'm not I am trying to be brave
yet I can feel the tears fill my eyes
they lower the coffin into the hole
I throw some flowers down and start to cry
I miss you so much why did you have to die?
I remember when you were ill I was so sad, I felt for you
the nurses were nice to you and I know you made friends
we all miss you and we always will
goodbye Grandad, for now, forever.

***Suzanne Berrie (12)***
***Inveralmond Community High School***

## FLOWER

Burst into colour one day,
And liven up the place.
When that favourite flower of mine is out,
There's a smile on my face.

Come spring,
You shine and brighten up the gloom.
Sweet smells when you're in bloom.

During the winter months, were locked up all day.
But when you smile,
We know it's time to come out again and play.

***Jennifer Wilson (11)***
***Inveralmond Community High School***

## SEVEN SINS

I lean my body over white stone,
I balance myself over the lakes of mortality,
They're creepy behind me,
The seven deadly sins each stalk and prey.
I'm travelling fast and swiftly through the night,
Praying and hoping for a swift escape.
The seven sins are like beggars, scrounging off
People's souls and sucking them dry like a sponge,
Greed, betrayal, lust, anger, sloth, gluttony and
Jealousy are speeding up,
They are angry, very angry,
There is no means of escape,
The sins are like bloodthirsty hounds chasing me,
The poor defenceless fox which is speeding
Away from an untimely death of getting ripped to shreds
Like wet paper on the touch of a hand
I have defied them now they want revenge.
I am now leaping into the lakes of mortality.

***Nicole Suliaman (12)***
***Inveralmond Community High School***

## DARKNESS

Darkness is scary, darkness is weird,
The light goes off and darkness appeared.
Darkness squeezes under my bed,
Darkness hides all around my head.
It comes from the corners,
It comes from outside.
But when the light goes on,
It goes back to hide.

***Heather Kelday (12)***
***Inveralmond Community High School***

## Darkness

The thought of being blind, really really scares me.
The thought of living in darkness scares me even more

My best friend is blind,
She's been blind since birth,
All she sees is darkness,
Darkness all the time.

I ask her what she sees,
She said she's got a world,
Living in her head.
I sometimes sit and wonder
What she's on about.

She's captured in a zone of darkness,
That's what it's all about.

***Siobhann Pratt (12)***
***Inveralmond Community High School***

## Mr Nobody

He is the one that makes all the fingerprints on the window,
He is the one that leaves muddy boots in the hall,
He is the one that messes the bedroom when he comes to play,
But still my mum doesn't believe me when I say,
It wasn't me mum it was Mr Nobody.

He is the one that leaves dirty dishes in the sink,
He is the one that gets me into trouble for everything,
He is the one that shouts at my mum,
Not me!
I tell you it was Mr Nobody!

***Emma Bilston (11)***
***Inveralmond Community High School***

## The Girl

She sat alone by her window,
Feeling depressed and low,
As she does all day, every day.
Gazing out, saying nothing just looking out onto the bay.
She sees no purpose in life and hasn't one friend,
Wishing so much her life would end.
She hears the tapping of the rain,
Inside she feels a lot of pain.
At night she lies awake, her heart tearing apart with
Loneliness and sadness.
Only wishing for a brand new start.
Her mind is full of worry and fright,
Thinking she can't do anything right.
No one can understand her gloom,
Praying for her life to change soon.
Words can't express how she's feeling.
Soon she'll start dealing,
To find out what she's really feeling.
'Cause loneliness is too much to bear,
Especially when nobody cares!

***Fiona McAllister (11)***
***Inveralmond Community High School***

## Pup

One day old
Blind and new to the world
Lying on a cushion
The other pups all pushing
Legs are just like jelly
The cushion his mum's belly
With a breakfast bar built in.

***Jay Phillips (12)***
***Inveralmond Community High School***

## DREAMER

I'm just a boring old schoolgirl,
I'm not very bright at all.
So I have to pretend I'm someone else,
So that I don't feel so small.

The other day I was a pop star,
My face was on every magazine cover.
The press were always on my back,
I couldn't do one thing or t'other!

I soon escaped to become a writer,
Winning awards all the time.
But soon my good fortune came to an end,
Because I was no longer in my prime.

So I became a super thin model,
When it came to money I had the highest rate.
But soon my career began to plummet,
Because of the chocolate I ate.

I decided I'd done enough dreaming,
Nothing I tried seemed right.
I think I'm best at being a schoolgirl,
After all, I'm not that bright.

***Heather O'Brien (12)***
***Inveralmond Community High School***

## My Uncle Fred

My uncle Fred'a a vampire
And doesn't wear a hat,
And every time it's midnight
He turns into a bat.

So if you hear tapping
When you're tucked up in bed,
Don't pull the blind for you will find
It's my awful uncle Fred.

*Victoria Tulloch (12)*
*Inveralmond Community High School*

## Caledonia

Scotland is a bonnie land,
Scenery untouched by any hand,
With beaches full of golden sand
Where hills and mountains stand so grand,
Sweet water runs down the burns
And heather covers wee roads that turn
Through toons and glens and but and bens.
You'll take the high road
again and again.

*Paul Millar (12)*
*Inveralmond Community High School*

## POEM

I love playing football
I sometimes play in the gym hall
Now and again I fall
As I try to do tricks with the ball.
Sometimes I score
My friends call for more.
As I pass the ball along the floor
I look at the door
I see someone pour

Juice.

*Half-time!*

There are eleven players on our team
Our strip is maroon and cream.
When we win our faces beam
We want to see a trophy gleam
Come on my team!

*Full-time!*

***Grant Cairns (13)***
***James Gillespie's High School***

## KATIE

She is cold like the winter snow,
She is like a wild cat, with paws as sharp as saws.
She is like a glass of lemon juice, cold and sour,
She is like the planet Pluto, far from the sun.
Her hands are like cats' claws.

***Zenab Sharif (12)***
***James Gillespie's High School***

## WOLF

I am a frosty winter day.
I am fire and wind sweeping through the trees.
I am the basement all dark and scary.
I am a Porsche all sleek and shiny.
I am an innocent criminal on the run.
My voice is loud being heard everywhere.
My eyes are coal black and fiery.
My paws and claws are sharp and long.
I am a spear slicing through the air.
My fur is soft like a kitten.
My ears are small but pointy.
My teeth are earthquakes fast and shaking.
I am a thunderstorm on the roll.
I am a cymbal crashing loud and long.
If I don't watch myself I will be next year's winter coat.

***Anika Ludwig (12)***
***James Gillespie's High School***

## THE BEACH

The beach lies stretched before us like a quiet, peaceful lawn in summer.
The sun blazing down on the sea, lapping up the shore, like a cat drinking milk out of a dish.
Then running down to the edge.
Its footprints in the sand waiting to be washed away.

***Hannah Thomas (13)***
***James Gillespie's High School***

## I Am A Tiger

I have all the time in the world,
never needing to go home.
I have freedom,
more freedom than William Wallace.

My jaws are giant can crushers
crushing cans with ease.

My legs are giant tree trunks
that can't be broken.

I'm a car my fuel
is the blood of other animals.

***Billy McCallum (12)***
***James Gillespie's High School***

## Giraffe

I am the top floor
I am the wind glaring down on everything it passes over.
I am a long thin spiralling carrot
I am a flute playing low, soprano notes
I am a woollen jumper with holes and patches.
I am muddy water drunk by an old man through a windy straw.
My teeth are chunky warehouses
My smile is a grim and dopey line
I am an unemployed tramp
My hooves are chunky U turns
I am a run down rusty wreck travelling slowly and
Elegantly across the dusty plains.

***Steven Hanton (13)***
***James Gillespie's High School***

## The Man And His (Moon) Walk

Like winter, natural and beautiful,
Joyful for many,
Yet treated so coldly.

An innocent rat,
Locked in a cage,
Forever caught,
And cruelly hurt.

Less of a real plant,
More a child's drawing.
Forever changing,
But beautifully simplistic.

His eyes are the sea,
Beautiful, unexplored,
Dreadfully overlooked
And full with the innocence
Of a child's heart.

***Samuel Gieben (12)***
***James Gillespie's High School***

## My Best Friend

She is like summer, bright and happy.
She is like a hyena, amusing and sly.
She is a tough but rare steak.
Like Blackford Hill, she is independent and strong.
She is like night, alive but sleepy.
She is powerful like a lion in his pack.
Like a drum she's the main beat of a band.
She's a cat friendly but aware.
Like the sun she's radiant.

***Kate Weston (13)***
***James Gillespie's High School***

## HUMFFLETTA MY HAMSTER

I am small sweet and loving, always there, omnipresent
My legs are twigs, sturdy, strong but fragile
My eyes are jet, deep shiny and thoughtful but full of life
My body is a shell, protective hard and gritty
I am full of life, bouncy and unclear
I am quite small but precious
I am a small harp, delicate but playing the softest melodies
I play the smallest part in the strands of life.
I am autumn, sleepy and drowsy, but when awake frantic
I am a mule, determined, I never give up, always trying my best
I never stop a task until it is fulfilled
I am a camel, storing my supplies, using them little in my
desert surroundings.

***David Redpath (13)***
***James Gillespie's High School***

## LION

I'm fire - everybody is scared of me.
My hair is a bush.
My teeth are sharp pen-knives.
I'm whisky, strong and firm.
My eyes are magnifying glasses big and staring.
My paws are spades to scoop up my prey.
I'm a plane roaring along the runway.
I'm the drums very loud.
I'm a hurricane crashing through the jungle.

***Michelle Rafferty (12)***
***James Gillespie's High School***

## THE PANTHER

I am a detective dark and mysterious
My eyes are emeralds shining and sparkling
I am the most graceful of all ballerinas
My fur is black velvet varnished and smooth
I am a rich woman's most prized evening jacket
I am water flowing calmly
I am a limousine dark and rich
I am everyone's shadow
I am the most cunning of killers
I am a study serious and informative
I am a cyclone unexpected yet powerful
My teeth are Dracula's fangs.

***Krishma Bachoo (13)***
***James Gillespie's High School***

## SNAKE

I'm the fire of the jungle, quick and raging.
I'm a hurricane, free and deadly.
I'm a shed, standing on my own in a desert.
I'm a motorbike speeding along a winding dirt track.
I'm July, dry and wicked
I'm a coat worn by wealthy murderers.
I'm whisky, a burn on the throat.
I'm maracas shaking to a rumba beat.
I'm a mushroom, poisonous and dangerous.
I'm a prisoner collapsed on a stone floor.
I'm a lemon, bitter and twisted.

***Stephanie Campbell (13)***
***James Gillespie's High School***

## Poem About Peebles

I go to Peebles every weekend,
I go with my dad and a friend,
We leave Friday at five,
And down to Peebles we drive,
The caravan is where we stay,
Dad reads his book, while I go to play (snooker)
I have loads of friends I meet in the park,
There's Kevin, Fiona, Neil, Marcella, Louise
and Mark,
I go home after swimming on Sunday,
but I would like to stay,
but I have school on Monday,
When I get home, I realise I have a stack of
homework to do,
After a cool weekend I've a lot to get
through!

***Patricia Lamb (13)***
***James Gillespie's High School***

## Schooldays

The schooldays are too long!
The teachers always have to moan.
The toilets always smell of a horrible pong.
There are always good days and bad days,
subjects like French, science but then the bell
always goes 'Ding dong.'
At break meet with friends or go to the canteen.
Then back inside to be bored to death,
and the rooms are so stuffy you can hardly get a
fresh breath.
I am sure the rules are made to suit the teachers!

***Derek Donaldson***
***James Gillespie's High School***

## BULLYING

You think you haven't hurt me
With those long, evil glares
If you knew how upset I was
You still wouldn't care.

You like being nasty,
You like being cruel,
You're trying to impress your friends
You think you're being cool.

I see you in the corridor
You give me a hateful look
I feel so down and alone
All my confidence you took.

How could you do this to me?
How could you be so unkind?
My life is a misery
But you think that I don't mind.

You sit behind me in the classroom
And make a spiteful remark
It feels like a knife's gone through me
So sore, painful and sharp.

You may be the winner now
As your sick ways have gotten to me
But this will not always be the case
As stronger than you, one day, I will be.

***Jennifer Hogg (13)***
***James Gillespie's High School***

## NATURE

The jungle is mysterious.
Around every corner reaps another
surprise that just might kill.

But nature must reap its
fury on something,
lions wait to pounce on an
unsuspecting victim.

From jungle to island,
volcanoes and earthquakes
make governments fall to
their knees and must pay.
While the unprepared weep
over the dead.

The prepared are cautious.

Hurricanes are swift and
decisive to the unprepared.

People stampede out of town
at the last possible moment.
Their thoughts of a beautiful
home vanquished forever in
the realms of unhappiness.

***Colin Cavanagh (13)***
***James Gillespie's High School***

## Beth

There is no greater spell you can cast
No curse more unforgiving
I wish we could forget the past
I'll be in love with you until I stop living

    Just friends is a life sentence
    I'd rather be sentenced to death
    Whatever I did I'm forever repentant
    I'll always be in love with you, Beth.

Your eyes burn through and scorch my soul
My eyes see only one vision in black
I'm sinking deeper into an endless hole
I'll kill myself, babe, if I don't get you back.

***David Crabtree-Logan (13)***
***James Gillespie's High School***

## Cat

She moved silently through the undergrowth
She has lengthy claws, and velvety soft paws
    She arched her back
    And lifted her tail
A ripple shivered along her spine from the
    tip of her tail
A fire burned green in her vivid eyes
She jumped with grace, high into the air.
Down she came with a cry
She had caught a mouse!

***I A Harris (13)***
***James Gillespie's High School***

## THE MAN

Take the *man*;
He wishes to be Lord of Creation,
but cannot master himself.

Constantly seeking an explanation,
but unable to accept the answer,

He seeks order,
but revels in chaos.

He constantly gazes farther,
but does not look within.

He is petty, thieving and grabbing,
He is thankless, hateful and nagging,
He is noble, giving and kind,
He is gentle, joyful and refined.

Take the *man* . . .
but what is a *man?*

***Korshi Dosoo (13)***
***James Gillespie's High School***

## RAIN

Drip drop drip drop
goes the rain falling from
the cloudy sky to the
gloomy ground.
Puddles everywhere I look.
Splish splash of the
sound of the rain thumping
against the rooftops.

***Sallmah Abdulgader (13)***
***James Gillespie's High School***

## LION

I am summer dry and hot.
I am Africa wild and free.
I am fire burning through the plains.
I am the living room, I dominate.
I am the king or queen, I rule.
I am a French horn playing low notes.
I am a big warm jumper worn by a child.
I am a train fast and powerful.
I am wind sometimes calm and sometimes fierce.
My hair is the long dry grassy plains.
My teeth are daggers, sharp and deadly.
My voice is a foghorn loud and piercing.
My paws are killing machines.

***Bragela Hornal (13)***
***James Gillespie's High School***

## A SPELL TO MAKE YOU FLY

First into a cauldron black,
A liver to make you crack,
The taste of broccoli is so bad,
The sting of wasp makes me mad,
A drop of blood will add a bang,
Taste of spider adds some tang,
Snail will crawl into the pot,
Worms that wriggle freshly caught,
Brussel sprouts will make it worse,
An insect bite will make you curse,
If you wish upon this notion,
You will experience a flying motion.

***Craig Johnston (12)***
***James Gillespie's High School***

## MUM

My mum yells and screams all day
Making me listen to what she has to say
Telling me off and bossing me around
Making me pick my things up from the ground.
We go out shopping and I pick out my clothes
But everything I like, mum turns up her nose.
My mum still insists to take me out
Although we always end up having a scream
and shout.
Mum constantly tells me what to do
But I can never say 'Mum, it's you.'
'Wash your face and go to bed
You are giving me a sore head,'
Mum yells from the bath.
But I just snigger and start to laugh,
'I can't, you're in there' I reply.
Mum came out and gave a sigh
'Be quick you naughty child
Or I shall start to go wild.'
'Night mum, I'm going to sleep
Until tomorrow you won't hear a peep.'

***Loren McCauley (13)***
***James Gillespie's High School***

## FOR A WORLD OF PEACE!

In the cauldron boil and bake,
Love, peace, friendship wait!
Let the trees reach to the sky,
See the birds up very high.

Let's not see another bomb,
Make the wars be forever done.

Ample food for everyone,
Ground that's enriched by the sun,
From the east to the west,
Can we try our very best?

Let's not see another bomb,
May the wars be forever done!

***Kim Stephen (11)***
***James Gillespie's High School***

## SAY SHE'S A SNOB BUT I KNOW BEST

I look at her and I see what they mean.
With her nose in the air and her head held high
wearing her green-pea suit.
She occasionally wears her hair in plaits with short
green ribbons tied in bows.
Say she's a snob but I know best.
If you ask her 'What school do you go to?'
She will answer in her snobbiest voice
'St Margaret's' and after she will add
'Expensive too, you know.'
Say she's a snob but I know best.
Then after she will start to laugh her snobbiest
laugh which to me sounds like a horse.

Say she's a snob but I know best, she's
just like me and you.

***Sophie Macphail (11)***
***James Gillespie's High School***

## A Spell To Fill The World With Kindness, Friendliness, Hope And Peace

Use a cauldron big and black
to stir the potion nice and slack,
Which when spilt onto the ground
will explode and make a peaceful sound.

Gather up a family's love
and in it goes with a caring glove,
A huge jar of great affection
for love and warmth in every section,
A lump of warmly hopeful faith
which'll wipe out every wraith,
Then a load of tranquillity
mixed with hopeful ability,
Then you'll feed to the world and beings
kindness, friendliness, peace and hopeful hoping.

***Asma Majid (12)***
***James Gillespie's High School***

## Spell To Make You Rich

A rat's eye
Some hair from a fly
A lottery ticket
A one-penny piece
A lizard's head
A vicious beast
Mixed together with stewed beef
Bring to the boil and
let it simmer and
you are sure to be a lottery winner.

***Chris Phillips (12)***
***James Gillespie's High School***

## A Spell To Turn You Into A Cat

Stir boiling water into a pot.
Try not to make it too hot.

Add a black hair of a cat.
Stir it with a tail of a rat.
Steal a cat's-eye from the road.
Mix it in with a large toad.
Drop in a crystal so very bright
That cuts through the darkest night.
Add a fluffy white cloud.
Fire to make it explode so loud.
Add a leaf that you have found.
Stir it all around with a pound.

Drink when you see a bat
And you will turn into a cat.

***Michael Donald (12)***
***James Gillespie's High School***

## Witch's Brew

Boil, boil don't let this spoil
A drop of blood and a can of oil.
A frog's leg a bat's ear
I think this potion is something to fear.
The cauldron is nearly full
A tail of a cow and a horn of a bull.
A spider and web and a cockroach too
This is the end of my witch's brew.

***Stephen Moffat (12)***
***James Gillespie's High School***

## The Limerick Poem

There was a clever young lad named Jim,
Out in a car he went for a spin,
The car it did crash,
With a terrible smash,
And now he is rather quite dim.

There was a young girl named Pat,
Who went out and bought a white cat,
The cat caught a mouse,
Brought it into a house,
And Pat told the cat to scat.

A little young bird in a wood,
Under a tree he stood,
A conker fell down,
Right onto his crown,
Then he was in a terrible mood.

There was a young lass named Betty,
Who ate tons and tons of spaghetti,
One day she ran out,
No longer was stout,
No longer she looked like a yeti.

***Louise Brown (11)***
***James Gillespie's High School***

## Sorrow

Nowhere to run,
Nowhere to hide,
Nobody knows how I feel inside.

From all the horrors that I have met,
I may move on, but I'll never forget.

I have to be strong,
I have to be wise,
But deep in my heart, it all still lies.

Sometimes I feel it will never be eased,
It will not go until the tormentors are seized.

***Sepiden Golzari (13)***
***James Gillespie's High School***

## HAPPINESS

Happiness is when the sun shines on your face
Happiness is when you have a special place
Happiness is when you smile
Happiness is just half a mile
Happiness is full of light
Happiness is when you face your right
Happiness is when you laugh
Happiness is not very daft
Happiness can be your secret
Happiness can be your chocolate
Happiness is when you go out to play
Happiness is when you find your way
Happiness is like joy
Happiness is not when you get a toy
Happiness is when you're on holiday
Happiness can be quite a long way
Happiness can't be far
Happiness can be in Mars
Happiness is when you are happy
Happiness is when you are funny
Happiness is full of colour
Happiness is when you can be under cover
Happiness is happiness and that is what you are!

***Kanan Cheung (13)***
***James Gillespie's High School***

## WHY?

Why did it have to happen to her?
Why did they have to be so mean?
Why couldn't they see she'd never hurt them?
Why when she walked down the corridors did they have to glare?
Why did they have to stare at her with those piercing eyes?
Why did they have to start commenting, words like pounding hammers?
Why go on and on, and make her feel like dirt?
Why when all she wanted to do was die, did they keep on trying to make her cry?
Why did she start to cry when they came to say 'Hi?'
Why don't they just leave her alone and let it be?
Why don't they understand, she's had enough?
Why does it have to keep going on and on, being dragged up over and over again?
Why do all these things go through my head?
I know for sure that she will always be my friend!

***Lucy Warren (13)***
***James Gillespie's High School***

## A SPELL TO TURN PAGES

Two nimble fingers, one fat thumb,
Into the cauldron one by one,
Three white mice, and head of dog,
A fiery flame, and a mound of fog,
Leg of lizard, and wasp's sting,
Brain of human and alarm clock ring,
Pages of print and two eyes,
Head of human, make sure it dies.
Let the cauldron boil and churn,
It will be ready in a trice,
Pages will turn, isn't that nice.

***Ysolda S Teague (12)***
***James Gillespie's High School***

## POTION TO MAKE YOU GOOD AT FOOTBALL

Cheetah's speed, eagle's sight,
Kangaroo's foot, a will to fight
Giggsie's skill, Vinny's will,
A certain grace and lots of pace.

Mix this up in the pan,
with eye of newt and marzipan,
add wing of bat and fin of shark,
next to go a bit of bark.

Through the tunnel and onto the pitch,
lots of swearing and lots of spit,
then the players start to play,
oh what a game, we can't delay,
oh what is this that I can see,
it's super sub a-running free,
he finds the gap and takes the pass,
then strikes the ball,
it's in at last!

He'll not be on the bench next week,
right now he's playing at his peak.

Even though the game is over,
for seven days, we'll be in clover.

This magic potion has worked for him,
and now the league is theirs to win.

***Colin Pollock (12)***
***James Gillespie's High School***

## The Sun And Moon: As We Don't Know Them

The sun's rays are like golden hands, touching
the dew glittered land to gently wake it up.
She shines on us all day as she
drifts over the calm blue sky.
Watching as we get on with our fragile little lives.
In the evening she slowly glides
round the earth to brighten the lives
of strangers in other places.

The moon now greets us as he comes into view.
He glows like a white jelly bean, sucked
and glistening in a pool of black.
Stars are chattering and twinkling like
children in a playground.
They gossip and tell him stories which make him smile.
He knows the sun is coming and he is happy in the dark
So he slips away to make room for her brightness.

***Imogen H Alabaster (13)***
***James Gillespie's High School***

## My Sister

She is a tornado,
Pretty to the eye,
Deadly to the touch.

She is a synthesizer,
Like its many sounds,
She in turn has many different moods and ways.

Like a weeping willow,
Her hair is long and flowing.

She is a vampire on a Saturday,
Sleeping in the day,
Raving at night!

In the morning she is like a computer
Downloading the bible.

She lies like a journalist,
For she is my sister.

***Eddy Hackett (14)***
***James Gillespie's High School***

## The General

Hup one
Hup two
About face
Take aim
Fire!
Hup one
Hup two
Stand straight
Jones!
Get down
Give me twenty
Hup one
Hup two
Right
To the canteen
Double time
Salute
Dismissed.

***Stephen Morrow (12)***
***James Gillespie's High School***

## MY LAST DAY AT BRUNTSFIELD

We hugged our teacher, waved goodbye,
Walked out of the classroom, filled with gloom,
The classes were lined up, p3, 4 and 5,
Their clapping and cheering was loud and boomed.

I just couldn't face it, I held my head low.
Everyone was smiling - I was in tears,
I raised my glance upwards -
Fixed on the door.
Tried to block out the shouts and cheers.

We reached the staircase,
More children were there,
I couldn't believe it -
Why should they care?

Now it was the small ones,
P1s and p2s.
Their smiling faces -
Their teachers too!

We were out of the building, - a breath of fresh air.
Last of all the p6s, clapping and clapping.
I felt the wind blow through my hair,
I looked through the open gate, where
All my friends were standing.

My whole class was crying,
I couldn't believe it!
We wandered around comforting each other.
The school day was over-
Now the summer term.
Why were we upset?
I tried to find my brother.

Now we're in high school,
We still keep in touch,
But I'll never forget,
The day of so much.

***Lucy Young (12)***
***James Gillespie's High School***

## NIGHTMARE

The cold and lonely island
Lost and alone
Nowhere to stay
Nowhere to sleep
Clouds turning dark
Filled with rage and terror
Trees ganging up on me from either side
The wind searching for somewhere to stay
Rain pattering against the rocks
Lightning striking, blinding me with every flash
Thunder rumbling with anger
Waves racing to the shores
The wind searching and searching
Rain gushing and gushing
Lightning brighter that ever before
Thunder roaring and roaring
Beaches disappearing into the far distance
The sky filled with lights
Branches scattered along the mud
Trees uprooting
*Help!*
*Aaargh!*

***Sarah Afzal (12)***
***James Gillespie's High School***

## My Family

In my family there's my . . .

Dad, who is sport crazy,
Especially for football,
He eats non-stop,
And thinks he knows it all

Mum, always ironing, cooking
Doing something
Always dieting
And busy learning to drive.

My sister, very annoying,
Playing the viola (squeaky)
Can hit, bite, punch, kick hard.
And never shares.

That's my family,
A bit on the mad side,
Over protective,
But I couldn't be without them.

***Julie Rudge (12)***
***James Gillespie's High School***

## Parents

'Do this, do that,' that's all they ever say,
Then they nag, nag, nag,
That I can't go out to play.

My dad is football crazy,
He won't miss a game,
Mum is often nice,
But she loves to complain.

Parents think they know what's best,
The truth is they don't have a clue,
They pretend they know it all,
But it's us kids who really do!

***Laura Kilpatrick (12)***
***James Gillespie's High School***

## POEM SCHOOL

I wake up in the morning,
And think everything's just cool,
Until my mum reminds me,
That I've got to go to school.

Eventually I get up,
Still very, very tired,
Get told to go and get washed and dressed,
And go to boring old school.

I consider playing truant,
To miss geography,
But in the end I decide to go,
For my teacher will take a ragie.

Stop at every sweet shop,
Trying to waste some time,
From the evil fate that awaits me,
For eight hours every day.

When I eventually get there,
I am really, really mad,
For you'll never guess what day it is,
It is, of course, a Saturday!

***Alan McDonald (11)***
***James Gillespie's High School***

## DENTIST

When I get to the dentist,
I get onto a movable chair,
I smell the anaesthetic,
And I wish I wasn't there.

When I visit the dentist,
They talk about me having braces,
When they give me one,
I make lots of horrible faces.

When I get to the dentist,
Because I am missing school,
I'm not very well pleased,
I am missing going to the swimming pool.

When I get to the dentist,
I get some teeth pulled out.
And if it isn't for the dentist's hand,
I would have to shout.

When I get to the dentist,
I am in extreme pain
I am getting fillings,
It is also starting to rain.

When I go to the dentist,
I do not want the electric drill,
I would rather cry,
Or go running half way up a hill.

When I got to the dentist,
My heart is beating quicker,
I am only having a check-up,
But am getting rewarded with a sticker.

***Morna Royden (12)***
***James Gillespie's High School***

## DREAMS

When you're dreaming you're in your own little world,
Nobody to disturb you or to spoil your thoughts,
Your thoughts can be either good or bad,
But you can always awaken but not always forget.

Dreams can be about a fire or a storm,
or a chase when you're the victim,
Maybe imaginative like you're a whale or a bird,
Or memorable like a killing.

As you snuggle under your covers
Attempting to keep warm and content,
Trying to forget all the thoughts you've just had,
But they're still swarming about in your head.

As I drift off to sleep again,
Thinking of a summer's day,
I look down and there's a spider there,
The image won't go away.

In my dream I can hear someone shouting,
I look around but no one is there,
There it is, the shout once again,
Who is it? Oh, I don't care.

My bedroom door is opening,
All those dreams have gone,
As I get up unwillingly,
I remember the night being long.

***Katherine Hopkins (13)***
***James Gillespie's High School***

## The Weather In Paradise

As the wind blows through the trees,
It seems as if the leaves are bullets
Firing from a gun.

The grass was blowing in the compasses
North direction.
All this because of the wind!

The rain beats down on the window-panes,
Trying to get in on me,
If it wants to come in or me to go out,
It will have to give in to the sun

Hot and still,
Burning through my skin,
Will it give in?
As I slap on the sun-cream and swim in the pool,
The sun creeps behind the clouds.

Cotton balls stuck to a painted blue sky,
Are pushed around by the wind.

As the sun sets in, all this is gone covered in dark black.
Now the moon and stars rule this wonderful paradise.

***Jenny Avern (13)***
***James Gillespie's High School***

## I Want . . .

Hi, mum. Want a cup of tea?
Here's the control, now watch TV,
Put your feet up on this chair,
And by the way, I like your hair.

There's something I want to ask,
About a few things that I'd like.
Don't worry, they are not too expensive,
And no, it's not a bike.

I want a TV in my room,
Why not? I'm thirteen,
All my friends have got one too,
Ooh mum, you are mean.

Well, how about that jumper,
Ted wore today,
The one he got for his birthday,
It's blue, maroon and grey.

He said it cost him thirty pounds,
Half price during the sales,
And how about some new trainers,
The Reebok ones like Dale's.

OK, you win, I've had enough,
I give up, I retreat,
But here comes dad, there's still a chance
To get a jacket like Pete's.

***Evan Holm (13)***
***James Gillespie's High School***

## When I Went Back

The winding mud track twisted round to the house,
The golden trees swayed in the autumn breeze,
The house towered over me like a burly giant.

I opened the groaning door like an old man in pain,
My shoes tapped on the tiled floor,
A gust of wind blew shut the door.

The cold silence of the eerie house was shattered by the squeal
of a mouse,
My whole body froze from head to toe,
Nowhere to hide,
Nowhere to go.

After plucking up the courage I walked up the stair,
I turned round for a moment,
Should I dare?
The door had not been open,
Yet the door had not been locked,
I wondered for a moment, perhaps I should have knocked.

I knew I was being stupid, no one was here,
No one was around, my gran had died last year.

Quietly I walked into her room,
For me it was like her empty tomb,
Every one of her ornaments was still there,
Even the red woven cushion still sat on the chair.

For me it was as though nothing had changed,
She could have been sitting there, her head full of curlers all
neatly arranged,

I couldn't take it any more,
I was going to cry,
Why was it, my granny had to die?

***Elise Andrews (13)***
***James Gillespie's High School***

## JUST DREAMING

When the teacher asks
I'm just dreaming
Dreaming of faraway lands
Dragons, elves and goblins.
I could be anywhere, any time.
Like I could be a climber in Tibet
Or a window cleaner on the Empire State Building.
But when it's all over, I'm in a classroom
After all, I'm just dreaming.

***Ravi Carothers (13)***
***James Gillespie's High School***

## OH ONLY . . .

'Do you want a cup of tea, or
maybe a cream bun?
Or how about a bar of chocolate?
I'll go to the shops and get you one.'
'What do you want now?'
'Oh only a new mountain bike,
pair of shoes, CK one . . . oh, why not, Mum!'

***Ellan Glen (12)***
***James Gillespie's High School***

## SWEET DREAMS

I walked past it every morning, every afternoon
On the way to and from school
Its doors were always open
I could see them lying there.

I asked my mother every day, every single day
The answer was always *'No!'*

I used to ask my friends at school,
'Just a bit, a tiny bit.'
'No,' they said, 'it's mine.'

Ah, but when the weekend came,
I would get my pocket money.

Out of the door I would rush
And guess where I went?
Straight up the road to the sweet shop
To view the sweets and pick my favourite.

I would hand over my money and leave.
As soon as I was out of the door
I'd open my sweets and stuff my face.
By the time I got home, they were gone.

***Lisa Morrison (12)***
***James Gillespie's High School***

## May There Be Peace

Please! Please! The kindness I pray,
Where has it gone?
Has it hidden away?
Where's that panda with the bamboo shoot,
And that dodo with the nice soft fur.

A peaceful sound,
A harmless ray,
A *bang*, that can't be right,
It can't be enjoyment,
It can't be the misty moonlight,
Please don't turn this into a fight.

The 19th century,
A walking protest,
The love of an unwanted red rose,
The dew,
The petals,
But yet the beauty and shyness,
The silent dream,
The secret goal to hope and long for,
The chance so distant it looks.

***Kate Lang (12)***
***James Gillespie's High School***

## From Where I Sit

From where I sit
I see the world
As it slowly turns
And life uncurls.

From where I sit
I see the lives
Of children, husbands
Siblings, wives.

Though destruction
Reaches far and wide,
I envy then
For living lives.

If I could only
Hear the sea
And feel the sun
Shine down on me

But from where I sit
I cannot leave
I must slowly watch life
As it weaves.

***Laura Bonsall (12)***
***James Gillespie's High School***

## A LOVE SPELL

Light the fire, stir the pot,
Give it everything you've got.
Leaf of rose and violet petals,
Gold and silver, precious metals.
Chocolate heart and diamond ring,
A rhyme to make his heart go ping.
A secret wish, a cupid's dart,
A spell to capture someone's heart.
A lovebird's song, a silver moon,
The wind whistling a lovely tune.
Light the fire, stir the pot,
Give it everything you've got.

***Sarah Wrigley (12)***
***James Gillespie's High School***

## TINY

I like to stroke my little dog
His name is Tiny Tams
He is soft and cuddly
And he likes to lick my mum.

He sleeps with me each night
And I hold him tight but he doesn't bite
His coat is black and white
And his tail is very bright.

***Elizabeth Tams (14)***
***Kingsinch School***

## THE BOY WHO DISAPPEARED

The boy went in the woods
In a bad mood
His friends were scared
Things weren't looking good.

His mum was upset
Asking where he was
His friends couldn't tell her
Because they had a bet.

They must not tell the secret
Where the garden hut was
If they do, what happens?
Their friend could be hurt or cross.

The next day they went to the gang hut
To see if he was there
He was reading in the corner
As if he didn't care

They took him home to his dad
His dad gave him a row
But really he was glad
To see him safe and sound.

***Sean Smith (14)***
***Kingsinch School***

## FISH

My pet fish makes me dizzy
They swim around in a tizzy
They play hide and seek
Come up for a breeze
And go back down again for a sleep.

***Michael Davidson (14)***
***Kingsinch School***

## My Sister

My sister's name is Jade
She's cool and neat
Whenever I walk out of the door
She bangs and kicks and greets.

She does some funny things
Like stealing mum's dinner and drink
She hits the dogs
She grabs the fish
She doesn't really think

Her hair is blonde
She's one year old
Her eyes are blue
She's cute
I really, really like her
She's definitely a beaut.

***Bernadette Boyd (13)***
***Kingsinch School***

## White Wolf

White wolf chased the big dog
Into the woods and into the bogs
White wolf got caught in the trap
Big dog got lost in the fog
He couldn't find his way home
So he slept in a tunnel made of stone.

***Colin Kwok (13)***
***Kingsinch School***

## LOTTERY OF LIFE

Circles tracing, undefined
The visible pallor left behind
Though unobstructed they search for the unburied treasure
Maintaining the need for a greater pleasure
Hindrance encourages their will to discover
Their security now, like the embrace of a lover
A saviour to change, to transform the times
New light will flood at the striking of the chimes
Mystery solved, clues scattered wild
Playing through the wind like the ghost of a child
Anticipation, grasping, the greed overwhelms
Searching through granite for the marble realms
Affection of the pity, perfection of the grace
Soon to be abolished at the winning of the race
Looming questions shall disappear
Unhappiness ebbs away, dragging with it, fear
Discontentment, dissatisfaction, lose their first three letters
The ultimate receipt, discharging debtors
Generosity grows, complacency alert
Just one last bet on the eternal dead cert'
Popularity explosion, new friends found
Liquid expenditure, pound by pound
Awareness shattered when the storm breaks
Pebbles of realisation thrown in sleeping lakes
Rich clouds clear leaving poorer skies
Isolated souls with tear-filled eyes
The dream came true, but eventually lied
Last hope lived, last hope died
Lessons learned, regrets forever
Adaptation back in time, memories of a beggar.

*Dawn Louise Turner (17)*
*Portobello High School*

## Enwrapped In His Spell

A magical stillness,
Wondering in an enchanting dream,
My mind is high-flying,
In the soft fluffy clouds,
he stares,
deep into my eyes,
seeming to see right through me,
I am bewitched, amazed.
Enwrapped in his spell.

The fascinating silence hypnotised me,
What is he thinking?
Is it about me?
He gets up and leaves,
I still sit there charmed,
I am left entranced, spellbound.
Like a victim of a love potion.

***Sarah McMahon (12)***
***St Augustine's High School***

## The Witch's Night Out

The witch's cape swept through the air
Ready to make the most daring of dares.
She cackled,
She snorted
She screeched with delight
As she was ready to give someone a fright.
Casting her spells up so high
Roaming through the dark night sky.

***Katie Mulgrew (12)***
***St Augustine's High School***

## THE WOMAN'S STORY - MIDNIGHT

All alone with the memory of him
So many foolish questions, as many as the stars above me.
His eyes gleamed.
Showing the reflection
of the happiest girl in the world.
I can still feel his soft hair
My eyes are stinging with piercing tears
He left me.
For the witch's daughter
She enchanted him with her mother's spell
Tears trickled down my cheeks, making them moist,
like the rose petals he gave me.
Now scrumpled on the grass
I'll never see him again.

The witch's daughter, like a black widow
Spinning her web,
Round more and more young men,
Capturing them with her beauty
Telling them how much she loved them and then
Sending them to their death
in the murky depths of her seabed,
So many young men's graves.

***Mairi Beaver (12)***
***St Augustine's High School***

## THE DARK NIGHT

It was a dark and misty night
When I saw a light
On top of the hill
Then there was a
Bright light
With a *bang!*
Then all was quiet.

Suddenly I saw a witch
Chasing me
So I ran and I ran
But the witch was getting closer
Then she got me
And killed me.

***Mark Walkingshaw (12)***
***St Augustine's High School***

## The Mystical Experience

I was hypnotised.
I tried to look away.
But I could not.
The softness of the bright yellow
eyes were hidden by the sharpness.
I could feel the cat's movement.
Coat as black as ebony wood.
Sleek as a black sports car.
Tail waving in the icy winter wind
like a scarf.
I could feel the magic in the air
I was fascinated.

As the world's day was ending.
My night was just beginning.
I knew the beauty of the cat.
Was to take me further through the
night.

***Ashley Miller (11)***
***St Augustine's High School***

## MAGICAL MIRACLE THOUGHTS

Magical, miracle thoughts enchanting me!
They drift through my head like a dream.

All the curious things my thoughts make up,
The feelings they give me,
happiness, sadness, movement and comfort.
It's nice having enchanting thoughts
spinning around and around,
as if they were spellbound.

And then one day
They vanished away
in a spark of light
But I know I was going to put up a fight.
With the person that stole my
magical, miracle, thoughts.

A mystic black cat
came with a bat
with magic at their side.
Where's my magic? Where's my charm?
What an alarm to have no charm

If you give me a stroke on the back
and a kiss for the bat
then I'll return your magic.
'OK' I say
And did as they asked.

A flash of light sparkled in my face
and slowly in a line like a song
The magic drifted along
into my ear and then once again it started
Those magical, miracle, thoughts.

***Catriona Appolinari (11)***
***St Augustine's High School***

## TRAVELLING THROUGH TIME!

Bored!
I sit in my room
Why is there no thrill?
Wow! I'm spinning round and round!
I'm travelling through time
I'm in 1943
World War Two is going on!
So why no guns or *bangs!*
Everything is spellbound in 1943
But then a shot!
It was a gun!
I've been shot
Why me?
I wish I was in my room being
Bored!
Than dying in World War Two
Spellbound! Why did you come?
You've made everything still
Except from a gun!

***Kieran Power (12)***
***St Augustine's High School***

## SPELLBOUND

Enchantment round me
        Like wizards shaking their wands
His magical smile
        Charming me.
Miracles come true,
        The only thing is
I don't think he likes me much
        But I love him so.

***Gemma Peirson (12)***
***St Augustine's High School***

## Spellbound

Witches making potions
Perfume, aftershave and beauty lotions
With eyes of newt, tails of cats
Dogs' tails and wings of bats.

Wizards casting lots of spells
Turning frogs into fish and frogs into shells
With his magic wand and pointed hat
He'll turn anything from a bird into a rat.

Ghosts and ghouls scaring like mad
They scare anyone, even your mum and dad
They fly 'cause they've no feet
Kids impersonate them using white sheets.

***Simon Thomson (11)***
***St Augustine's High School***

## Wizard

I think I'll be a wizard
You get a cool pointy hat
I'll muck about with spells
And turn my neighbour into a bat!
I'll make lots of monsters
And invite them round for tea
Afterwards we'll have a game of cards
And the winner will always be me!
When I reach 100
I'll retire from being bad
But I think I'll make one last potion
That will turn me into a young lad!

***Philip Turnbull (12)***
***St Augustine's High School***

## The Wicked Witch

Once I saw a wicked witch
In her little house
She was cooking
In her black cauldron

She went out on her broom
Flying high as a plane
Then I saw a girl
Beautiful like a star

I went in and freed her
And escaped like a robber
She came back with her magic wand
Zapped us like a shooting star

And cooked us for frog soup.

***David Li (12)***
***St Augustine's High School***

## The Fat Black Cat

I stood there with fear.
A big fat black cat.
Mystic and wonderful.
In its own little way.
Big black eyes
When you look into them.
It casts a spell on me.
With a hocus pocus.
Runs away, runs away,
Runs away with me.

***Tammy Duncan (12)***
***St Augustine's High School***

## FAIRIES, WITCHES AND WIZARDS

Fairies, witches and wizards
Enchanting things all around
The witch
her black cat and broom
flying higher and higher
all round the room.
And the wizard
his cape and his hat
making spells
using frogs' legs
and bats.
But then there's the fairy
the good little fairy
dancing around
with her magical wand
Fascinating,
Mystic,
Miraculous
Watching these things
is so fabulous.

***Nicole Pyper (12)***
***St Augustine's High School***

## THE MOONLIT NIGHT

I hear a scream
and run to look
out of my window
and there she was
with her black
wicked cat beside
her on the magic
broom.

Flying above the
moonlit castle
then down to the
cave of bewitch
and in her green
spooky hand she held
a red bag with
everything for
her poison to
make her powerful.

***Laura Sangster (12)***
***St Augustine's High School***

## HELP! WHAT'S THAT?

A spooky and eerie night
Only the moon shining bright
With the magical and mystical
breeze blowing by.

Suddenly I see something flying
in the sky
Is it a witch on a broomstick,
A wizard flying through the sky
Or a huge bat flying high

I am spellbound as to what I can see
It isn't a witch or can it be.
I stand there in fear, scariness is near
I feel cold and scared
It's coming closer to me
Flying down by the big oak tree
It's coming to get me . . .
*Aargh!*

***Siobhan Kane (12)***
***St Augustine's High School***

## SPELLS WITHIN

The cold air
The magical mist
How to contemplate such a feeling
I hear creatures of miraculous creation
I chant those words
Recite it to the air
No one can hear.

Now I stand
Entranced
Enchanted
Vision blurred with fascination
From the ground the mist everything moved
Fire and water swelled
The earth never to be the same
Now the spell complete -
It was him!

***Colleen O'Neill (12)***
***St Augustine's High School***

## SPELLBOUND

Spellbound by his smile
His face full of magic charm
Enchanted by him.
His glowing brown eyes
His looks cast a spell on me
He is so magical
His singing voice mesmerises me
His dance moves are spectacular
He's truly wonderful!

***Laura Doohan (12)***
***St Augustine's High School***

## Dancing Witches

Down in the valley
Late one night
4 or 5 witches
danced in the light.

I stood there spellbound
as they danced.
I watched enchanted
as they pranced.

As the heat rose high
those 4 or 5 witches
began to fly.
On their broomsticks
they went making magic.

***Natalie Jack (12)***
***St Augustine's High School***

## My Day-Dream

I looked up to the sky
And shut my eyes
His eyes sparkled like stars
And his smile enchanted me
I was spellbound.

When he brushed past me
It was almost like
*Magic*
His hair was blowing
Like silk in the wind

***Emma Soowamber (12)***
***St Augustine's High School***

## THE MYSTERY WITCH

If I was a witch
I would fly on a broomstick
Make all the money in the world
And run away to the planet Mars.
I would cast a spell on people
Eat what I want,
There would be no adults
Apart from teachers,
I would cast a spell,
It would go like this
Hocus pocus
Look at this
Change everything to be like this . . .
. . . Wonderful!

***Luisa Beatson (11)***
***St Augustine's High School***

## WITCHES AND GHOSTS

One Hallowe'en, witches and
ghosts came out to play.
They came from far and wide and
didn't want to hide.
Whish, whoosh and off they went
in and out of fences bent.
When dusk turned to dawn it was
time to go on and on till darkness
fell again.

***Claire Sutherland (11)***
***St Augustine's High School***

## Fire! Fire!

Fire, fire in the cave
Hot and glowing
I wanted to stay
I heard a laugh
I heard a scream
Then I saw a bloody scene.

***Matthew Fyfe (12)***
***St Augustine's High School***

## Witch

I think I'll be a witch
With a big pointed hat
Also with a bewitched black cat
I'll make everybody smell and itch
I'll ride up above with a big broomstick.

***Danielle Pagliarulo (11)***
***St Augustine's High School***

## Who Will Know

I wish I were a wizard to wear a pointed hat.
And tell my black cat to do this and that.
Trying to cast a spell, it's like magic
at the tip of your nose to the bottom of your toes.
Now no one else will get to know.
I will cackle, I will snort, I will kill that little wart.

***Janette Brown (12)***
***St Augustine's High School***

## ONCE I HAD A DREAM

Once I had a dream, I was in a witch's house,
She had a long nose and a tall pointy hat.

She had a big round cauldron in the middle of the floor,
She was stirring a potion.

She had a big book called 'Spellbound'
Spellbound, spellbound, spellbound
She was chanting, she was casting a spell.

I wondered what that spell was for.
I had no idea and I guess . . .
I'll never find out.

***Charlene Clark (12)***
***St Augustine's High School***

## WICKED WITCH

I want to be a wicked witch
and cast spells on a ghastly child
and see her cringe at my smile,

As her parents cry all night
I'll chain her down real tight
I may let her go not tonight or
perhaps tomorrow or at sunlight.

***Kasey McReynolds (12)***
***St Augustine's High School***

## WICKED AND WONDERFUL

Wicked and wonderful
that's how I am
I frighten in the night
and let it right out.

Everyone dies
and everyone scares
Pity it is not you who
is wicked and wonderful.

***Kirsty Muir (12)***
***St Augustine's High School***

## THE LITTLE WITCH

I take her here,
I take her there,
I take her everywhere,
She spoils my fun,
she goes on the run,
And she makes me play truth or dare.
She burns my stuff,
She thinks she's so tough,
and cooks my friends in a pot.
She chomps my frogs' legs,
She listens to Mystic Meg,
and she picks my little green spot.
Oh how I hate her,
She's always playing with her mummies
Oh how I hate her,
She always thinks I am a dummy.
But don't worry man,
I've got a plan,
She's going to be spellbound today.
Don't worry man,
I've got a plan
She's going to pay today.

***Terry Stewart (11)***
***St Augustine's High School***

## The Wizard's Wand

I want to be a wizard
And wave my magic wand,
I want to wear a magic cape
And cast a spell with my wand,
I want to poison people too
Entertain my own delights.
A broomstick I shall fly on
It will take me away all night.

***Catherine Goulder (12)***
***St Augustine's High School***

## I Wish I Was A Wizard

I wish I was a wizard I'd fly right to the sky.
I'd talk to all my witchy friends as they went speeding by.
I'd go to my old castle and make a magic spell.
I'd turn you to an ugly beast and you will never tell.
My magic is outstanding, I'd rule the vast dry land.
And if you're in a muddle, I'll lend an extra hand.
If I was a wizard I'd have lots and lots of fun.
I'd create all this sorcery until the morning sun.

***Christopher Keir (12)***
***St Augustine's High School***

## I Want To Be A Witch

I want to be a witch,
With my little black cat called Titch.
Sit on my wooden magic broom,
Hold on tight then zoom, zoom, zoom!
Turn upside down then take a swoop,
I try and try to loop the loop!

Tall, black hat and flowing cloak
Legs as skinny as a bicycle spoke.
Long, black, creepy hair,
People will turn round and stare.
And as I circle round and round.
They'll stare and gawp, spellbound.

***Lyndsay Lindores (12)***
***St Augustine's High School***

## A Witchy Dream

Their witchy looks mean no harm,
All they bother about is their charm,
Bursting their warts with entrancing snorts.
Brushing their hair with absolutely no care.
One or two casting a spell
So that they can look swell,
They know that people will scream,
But who cares, a dream's a dream.

***Lee-Ann Burns (11)***
***St Augustine's High School***

## Eerie

The wind moved,
The leaves crashed against the wall,
The tree echoed a thousand words,
The house lit up,
Everywhere was filled with the ghostly sounds,
The distant chanting started,
And suddenly disappeared,
The lights flickered and went out.

***Stephanie Boccoli (14)***
***The Mary Erskine School***

## A PARADE OF GLORY?

The banners waving to the trumpet cry
The crowds cheering as the men go by
Sun glistens on medals
Feet drum out a steady beat
A handsome soldier flashes a wink
And a girl blushes scarlet, pink
Another sees his parents there,
Standing proud and waving vigorously
They are sending their son to glory.
Polished muskets with sharpened bayonets
Are slung over uniforms which sparkle red, gold, blue.
Young heroes picture the battle zone
Gallant men falling for their country
Never to rise again
Voices, straining to be heard over the blast of cannons
As one boy comforts a dying friend
He listens to tales of a long lost love.
For that is what they really are.
Merely boys
As rain splashes on the gay parade
It reminds people of the tears that will splash on
these children's lives.
Far off a child begins to cry
You fools, you are sending them all to die.

***Veronica McLean (14)***
***The Mary Erskine School***

## The Loss Of A Family

It started with a rumble,
And one searchlight
I saw a dog fight as I ran
Ran to shelter
Gas mask and all
We ran but all was gone
I made for safety
Closely followed by another explosion
This time too close for comfort
Screams echoed in the night
But still I ran faster, faster
Until I reach safety
Only to find I fled alone.

***Fiona Patterson (12)***
***The Mary Erskine School***

## The Magic Kingdom

Deep down in the blue sea
Something's hidden from you and me.

A fairytale castle of floating weed
Where little shiny fish hide and feed.

Pink, pretty delicate shells
Sleeping chambers with chiming bells

Beautiful mermaids swimming in lines
The scales on their tails glimmer and shine

This is the magic in the blue sea
That you or I cannot see.

***Helen Wilson (14)***
***The Mary Erskine School***

## The Hungry Witch

With her long nose
And pointed toes,
She looks at her warts
And laughingly snorts,
'What a hideous beast I am
All I need now is a juicy frog to feast on!'

She went down to the bubbling bog
And caught her juicy frog,
She gulped it down quickly
And then felt rather sickly,
She felt like some meat
So she went out to find herself a child to eat.

She picked on a child
Who was running wild,
He was plump and small
With rosy cheeks as round as a ball.
He really was yummy
And good for her tummy!

She now felt very full
After all that gruel,
She felt quite ill
So she swallowed a pill,
'What a hideous beast I am
I don't think I'll be having anymore children to feast on!'

***Lindsay Paterson (12)***
***The Mary Erskine School***

## SPELLBOUND

Coloured stars
whirled through timeless
space,
Blue, pink, green and silver,
Orange grass grew lush
beneath
the oppressive scarlet sky,
Light-hearted swirls
of golden
light weaved quickly through the giant
purple marshmallows.
A Technicolor pig
S
w
o
o
p
e
d
through the air, as a hungry mouse
*pounced* on a petrified cat with blue
blood spurting from its veins.

*In a manic world*
she stood

*Spellbound*

***Laura Melville (14)***
***The Mary Erskine School***

## Mission To Titan

*(November, the year 2004)*

Titan, the undiscovered
about to be plagued by Earthlings.
Dusty plains, eerie rising vapours
This ancient world hides the
history of the twelve brothers
and sisters
- the clash of the Titans.

Draped in cloud the planet hangs
suspended in time, motionless as
the years sail by.
Now it is wakened from its slumber.

The memories of Zeus and his great
thunderbolt will be rediscovered.
The spell will be broken.
We will be spellbound.

Seven years away from Earth
an orange ball concealed in
the darkness and stillness of space.

***Jennifer Hunter (13)***
***The Mary Erskine School***

## Magic

Magic, magic, everywhere,
What does it mean?
Shooting stars and faraway places,
Witches, wizards, broomsticks and cauldrons,
Top hats, wands and white fluffy rabbits,
These are a few of my magical thoughts.

Magic, magic everywhere,
What is it?
Tooth fairies visiting and rainbow treasures,
Black cats crossing and fairy dust sprinkled,
Spells cast and potions mixed,
These are a few of my magical moments.

***Fiona Kerr (13)***
***The Mary Erskine School***

## THE MYSTERY OF THE VILLAGE

A special fairy came from beyond,
Gave the young girl a magic wand.
The wand was powerful and very strong,
The girl took care to do no wrong.

But suddenly one day the wand slipped and fell,
It put the whole village under a spell.
Everyone felt sleepy, tired and weak,
Nobody felt that they wanted to speak.

After a while, as time went by,
They just couldn't stay awake, no matter how they would try.
That was when the excitement began,
The fairies appeared out of the cupboards they ran.

They filled the street with music and song,
Wondering why they hid for so long.
The mystery of the spell was shown so clear,
By the fairies that had once lived in fear.

Now it was broken because the wand fell.
The fairies would waken the village to tell,
They had always stayed close by but were kept apart,
But now the spell was broken, they could make a new start.

***Wanduska Jack (13)***
***The Mary Erskine School***

## Hallowe'en's Here

Hocus pocus witch's brew
Have a trick or treat or two.

It will soon be Hallowe'en
Dress up just like Mr Bean
You could be a cat or a witch
But get the costume, quick, quick, quick.

The cauldron's brewing
The cat is fat
The witch is standing
with her big tall hat.

Only twenty days to go
Make a rhyme
Sing a song
Because Hallowe'en's not long.

***Clare Grieve (14)***
***The Mary Erskine School***

## Magic

Crash, bang, boom
The Great Houdini arrives

Crash, bang, boom
A rabbit appears

Crash, bang, boom
Coloured balls fly in mid-air

Crash, bang, boom
The Great Houdini disappears.

***Melissa Watt (14)***
***The Mary Erskine School***

## SPELLBOUND

Held captive by his charm.
I stared into his magical sparkling eyes which dragged me
Towards him like two attracting magnets.
The spell of love which he cast over me, blew me away like
A rough sea sweeps a ship towards the horizon.
Just to see him fills my heart with joy, I feel like I am sitting
On a perfect white cloud high in the clear blue sky.
This obscure obsession will not leave me alone, it is attached
To me like a child is attached to its mother.
He empties my heart of love for anyone else, he is like a
Single bright star in a dark sky full of lights.
Caught under this spell of love, he makes me cry heavy tears
Like raindrops falling on a deep red rose.
Trapped within this immense power of love, forever . . .

***Heidi Dresing (15)***
***The Mary Erskine School***

## STARS

Stars are more dazzling than anything
in the world. In darkness they are
candles in a cave. They shine with
dazzles and shimmers like a sparkler
at Hallowe'en. I love stars that shoot
across the sky, like a rocket that just
took off, that flies with grace, like
a ball of fire.
Above all, I love them because, they
light up the still night with their
scintillating light that glistens like a
burning fire.

***Nicola Gotts (12)***
***The Mary Erskine School***

## THE THIRTY-FIRST OF OCTOBER

Hooray, hooray it's Hallowe'en
All the witches to be seen,
Most are black, a few are green,
Hooray, hooray, it's Hallowe'en.

Witches fly around the sky,
Cackling laughter as they go by,
Swooping low, then way up high,
What a sight for a child's eye.

Bonfires crackle in the cold night,
Leaping flames burning bright,
Crackling wood on bonfire sights,
Spreading heat to great delight.

Grab your pumpkin nice and quick,
Eat your apples, don't be sick,
Some will treat, some will trick,
Treacle buns, take your pick.

Hooray, hooray, it's Hallowe'en,
Now no witches are to be seen,
No more black, and no more green,
Hooray, hooray, it's Hallowe'en.

***Emma Waterman (14)***
***The Mary Erskine School***

## THE STORM

Thunder crashes,
Lightning flashes,
Dark skies all around,
Waves are thrashing,
Rain is crashing,
Hard upon the ground.

Sheep are sheltering,
From the winds,
The gulls are screeching loud,

But this storm will soon be over,
The sun breaks through the clouds.

***Louise Finlayson (13)***
***The Mary Erskine School***

## THE NIGHT I FLEW

I see them at night
Giving people a fright
They look up at me
And I say I can't see.

They cackle and scream
I think it's a dream
Now I'm awake
I know they're not fake.

They come into my room
Each on their own broom.
They take me away
Not giving me a say.

They talk as we fly
Way, way up high
They'll drop me soon
As we fly past the moon.

It was a good night
We flew like a kite
I hope they'll come back
But not to attack!

***Amy Coles (13)***
***The Mary Erskine School***

## A GLANCE THROUGH THE WINDOW

She gazed at the sycamore tree from her window;
The tree with the legend she had always known,
She thought of the stories she had loved to be told;
The ones where the lady in white had flown.
The street light yellowed its branches,
Their crooked silhouettes could be seen.
She imagined the creaky, haunted branch
Where the hanging rope had been.
The wind made a quiet rustling sound
And the tree then suddenly froze . . .
The clock ticked to midnight, chimed twelve times;
The day finally drew to a close.
She rose to shut her curtains,
Dragging them along the rail,
When she suddenly saw the terrifying face;
So white, so dead, so pale.
She looked at the face from the window.
The face looked at her from the tree
As if it were to ask a question;
What could the question be?
The branches shook, but she froze quite still . . .
Spellbound
Held against her will.

***Jenny Grosset (14)***
***The Mary Erskine School***

## SPELLBOUND

At any time, in any place
you can be captured.
Lured towards him,
mesmerised by his deep eyes.

Caught in a second,
enchanted, enraptured forever.

You gently fall together,
whirling,
spinning,
reeling,
twisting.
In a magical, hypnotic trance.
Bewitched and bewildered.

From that first moment,
every sense is overwhelmed.
Fascinated by this new vision,
you are exuberant with happiness and tranquillity.

Emotions are released from deep inside.
You know this will be eternal.
An unbreakable magnetic force.
Bound together with the magic spell of love.

***Claire Thom (15)***
***The Mary Erskine School***

## Pigs

Pigs grunt more noisily
than anything grunts. In mud they are
wallowing
in a Shangri-La. They search out truffles
with snub noses and heads close
to the ground

I love pigs that grunt
like engines, that wallow
blissfully, that snuff rich scents
like a bloodhound.

Above all I love them because
they waddle around
balefully, sniffing
for food
with their upturned
snouts.

***Alison Davie (13)***
***The Mary Erskine School***

## An Everyday Witch

This old witch lives all alone
Everyday she sits at home
This one day she came alive
She swarmed this boy like a beehive

She cast a spell upon this child
Today she seemed to be very wild
She chants the spell over and over
Then she turned on the engine in her Rover

She takes the child up to a cliff
She threatens to throw him out adrift
She chants her chants and screams and shouts
But she never takes upon his pout

Now today the boy's at home
He sits there wondering all alone
He sits in the dark waiting for her
But all he hears is his cat's purr.

***Lorraine Alonzi (14)***
***The Mary Erskine School***

## Cats

Cats sleep in more places
than anything else
In a strange sort of way
they are like tigers in a jungle.
They pounce with power,
and perfect precision.
I love cats
that are sophisticated
like ladies in pearls,
that purr softly
like the constant stroking of a harp.
Above all
I love them because
they slink down alleys
like a model on a catwalk,
with their shoulders pressed back
and their heads held high.

***Lindsay Foster (13)***
***The Mary Erskine School***

## SPELLBOUND

His face appeared to me
there was something strange about his youth
a mysterious aura
colours of scarlet
his eyes lit up
he grew closer to me
every move he made, I watched
I couldn't detach my eyes from him
he moved toward me slowly
the closer he came
the faster my heart beat
his lips were moist
robust hands wrapped round my waist
I was in a world of passion
he drew closer and closer to me
I felt I was dreaming
but was I?
my mind was flustered
or was I spellbound by love?

***Laura Kerr (17)***
***The Mary Erskine School***

## MIDDLE AGES

Middle earth to Middle Ages
Young and old alike
Around the night-time fire
Tell tales of days gone by

Of wizards and witches
making potions and spells
Hobbits and goblins
Fairies and elves

Knights in shining armour
Doing good deeds
Sitting up high on their big
valiant steeds

Dragons flying high up in the clouds
Breathing fire and brimstone out of their mouths
Oh what an adventure to have lived long ago
To see the bold dragons put on such a show.

***Jennifer Osborne (14)***
***The Mary Erskine School***

## DOLPHINS

A glint of assurance in a placid sea of despair,
A dolphin slices through the water unconstrained,
Its polished, streamline body, a splendour rarely seen,
With a soul of innocence only captured,
By a maiden of yesterday.

It welcomes in the lustrous, deep, sunrise,
Like a lost child reuniting with its mother,
They twist round like a never nding hurricane,
Its soft welcoming eyes tell a story,
That ancestors told before.

Dolphins merge together in a line, like can-can dancers,
Performing not for an audience, only for the watery sun,
The sea is now full of hope, like a scene from a fairytale,
Shades of pink and lilac invade the cyan,
The night is near, the dolphins repose.

A glint of assurance in a placid sea of despair.

***Samantha Millar (13)***
***The Mary Erskine School***

## Sunset Across The Horizon

Even before sighted, I felt its presence.
Hairs on the back of my neck, straightened,
Limbs tingled.
I turn, knocked back by its immensity.
As eyes are stretched apart,
Sucked towards it, I gasp.
In an hypnotic trance I obey,
In limbo between reality and fantasy.
Like a disease it seeps through me,
I put up no defences, there is no point to resist.
I am taken.
Muscles move involuntarily,
I have no control beyond it.
My soul given over, captivated.
forgetting troubles, stress, life
I float dreamily into bliss.
But perfection cannot last forever,
In a split second I hurtle towards Earth -
Speechless I recover.
The sight passed, but never forgotten
Until next time, when once again I will be -
Spellbound.

***Naomi A B Johnston (16)***
***The Mary Erskine School***

## Eyes

Eyes are more amazing than anything else.
In a way they are spectacular,
a show of colour in a world of dullness.
They open with expectance and
flicker with surprise.

I love eyes that glisten like crystals,
that shimmer like butterfly wings,
that glow like fairy lights.

Above all I like them because they
tell stories with their long
luxurious lashes.

***Lauren Donnelly (12)***
***The Mary Erskine School***

## SPELLBOUND

Walking along,
Turned the corner,
Silence.
Heartbeat quickens,
Standing motionless,
Eyes filled with amazement,
Awe and fascination.
Not being able to believe,
Stunned by its beauty,
Immobile, like being hypnotised.
Can it be real?

Running now,
Getting closer,
Stumble,
Caught up by my astonishment
Realising the object of my desire,
The spellbinding vision,
Had left my sight forever.
Heartbeat slows,
Back to normality,
Will I ever feel this way again?

***Kirsty Lind (16)***
***The Mary Erskine School***

## Abracadabra

His hand slowly enters the black hole.
The children's faces light up with excitement.
All the parents look up with anxiety.

Slowly, the hand emerges from the black hat.
A river of chirps and giggling flows through the room.
There is a moment of pushing and struggling in the hat,
And then appears a pair of long white ears,
A twitching nose,
The thumping feet,
And a cotton tail.

Abracadabra, the magic rabbit appears from the black hat.

***Magali Tuke (14)***
***The Mary Erskine School***

## Witches' Song

All the witches on Hallowe'en,
Gather to make a splendid scene.
Crowded round a huge, bubbling bowl,
Waiting to taste a little boy's soul.

One witch cackles which starts them all,
One after the other they start to call:
'Hallowe'en is here. The children are all fat,
Please put a big one in my crooked hat.
If you haven't got a big one a small one will do,
If you haven't got a small one, then I'll eat you.'

***Julie Mackenzie (14)***
***The Mary Erskine School***

## SPELLBOUND

The crowd focuses on the spinning bright colours
All watching the glared shiny eyes
Being tricked like a child

The magician mumbling a rhyme or two
Waving around his big black cloak as he pranced around the stage
Shouting, then whispering, then mumbling

With a click of a thumb
Silence
The crowd all silently sat still
Waiting for their first command

Waiting like a hawk would do for its prey
A command
One started dancing, then laughing, then, just sat down
All under one bad spell
All gullible
Guinea pigs

Another thumb click
A thunder of applause
As if rehearsed and timed correctly
but due to a silly spell
Which messes the mind of a human
but due to a man who is spellbound.

***Karen Black (16)***
***The Mary Erskine School***

## SPELLBOUND

Eyes flicker up and down,
People watch in admiration,
Incense wafts through the arches,
Colours merge as one.

The figure suspended high above,
Highlighted by the sun,
People stand transfixed.
To the man who preaches love.

The harmonious sounds float,
As we sing to the symbol above
Emotion fills the congregation,
The assembly is brought together as one.

Candles flicker in unison
With the one breath of the community,
Within the walls of sympathy and affection,
They give themselves to this faithful day.

Minds of the congregation,
Think as one towards the fascination
Of the preacher who is on high,
They bow to the charm of his voice.

***Hilary Bruff (16)***
***The Mary Erskine School***

## THE FANTASY TENNIS MATCH

As I walked onto the court
I had a very awful thought
It struck me down and made me frown
The thought that crossed my mind
Was that I had left my rackets behind.
It didn't seem like my lucky day
She tossed the ball it was time to play
I hit a forehand off the frame
I hit the next one just the same.
Five all forty love
And the rain came from above
The balls were heavy
And net-cords, ever so many.
My backhand was going very well
But only for a short spell
I hit my slice to keep it low
Then I won five games in a row
I used my topspin to create more pace
Then my opponent she lost the place
She began to shout and swear
'I'm playing rubbish it's just not fair.'
I was playing very well indeed
And managed to increase my lead
At 5-1, I served for the match
But my opponent hit a purple patch
Very soon it was 5-4
I thought 'I can't miss any more'.
I finished the match with a forehand winner
And jogged home to have my dinner.

***Frances Hendry (11)***
***The Mary Erskine School***

## UNDER A SPELL

*U* nder the spell of evil.
*N* owhere to escape to.
*D* evious and deadly.
*E* veryone's a victim.
*R* unning away won't work.

*A* ctually it will make things worse.

*S* pirits and demons arising.
*P* ray for some help they say.
*E* ven though they know it wouldn't work.
*L* et this not be true you say.
*L* ast chance, you're too late, the spell is upon you
now.

***Bita Jahan (14)***
***The Mary Erskine School***

## THE STAR OF THE SHOW

As she stepped onto the stage,
Like a swan into a pond,
She glided, swiftly, flying.
As the music coiled and curled
She felt it as it swept her in,
She noticed nothing else,
If she had felt anything,
She might have seen
The glare of the lights,
The heads in the crowd,
The jealousy in the wings,
The jealousy, which caused,
The slip of the silent swan.

***Karen McKerrow (14)***
***The Mary Erskine School***

## Apples

Apples are more juicy than anything in the world.

On a hot summer's day, they are more invigorating than a Coke would ever be.

They shine with pride that tempts you to bite them.

I love the juice that trickles down the skin like a raindrop that glistens in the sun, that refreshes me like a swim in a cold, deserted lake.

Above all, I love them because they taste delicious, and when you crunch them, they sound like the sky falling with their sweetness and delight.

***Catherine Brown (12)***
***The Mary Erskine School***

## Why?

I crouch, sweating and forced to one side.
The Anderson shelter shakes
As a bomb explodes,
No more than a mere two metres away.
Cries and shouts
Mice scamper about,
Tear stained clothes,
Bloody knees.
We were lucky this time.
What next?
Why go through with this?
Always on the edge and always so close.
Why?

***Catriona Morrison (14)***
***The Mary Erskine School***

## MERRY MOUTHING

I love mouths:
Those that glitter and those that are
grim.
They can change from laughter to
anguish, immediately.
They are the actors on the stage.
They tell a thousand stories;
The past, the present and the future.
They are the ruler of life:
The mute are the pained,
The linguistic; the happy.
Mouths have the ability to morph from
shape to shape,
And colour to colour.
Those that glitter are those that talk.

***Joanna Barcroft (13)***
***The Mary Erskine School***

## DARK NIGHTS

The night was empty
Still with no movement
The night was humid
Wet and damp
The night was electric
Fireworks bursting up everywhere
The night was red
Bonfires lighting up the sky
The night was still
Not a single leaf blowing in the wind.

***Vicky Smith (13)***
***The Mary Erskine School***

## A Silly Witch

There once was a witch
Who wasn't very bright
She tried and she tried
To get the spells right.

All day and all night
Zapping her fingers
Trying to find
Anything that lingers.

She hung up her hat
On the crooked hook
She found the secret
Inside her magic book.

So off she flew
To find a boy
To cast a spell on
His name was Roy

She changed some words
That were short and sweet
Poof she was gone
Apart from her feet.

***Gemma Kingsford-Smith (14)***
***The Mary Erskine School***

## The Witches Of The land

Deep in the valley,
Noises were heard,
Cackling and chanting,
Trouble being stirred.

I saw what I feared,
Fire roaring high,
Witches I saw,
Demons in the sky.

A small boy appeared,
A helpless cry,
Capturing his soul,
Why this cruelty, why?

***Kate Sheerin (14)***
***The Mary Erskine School***

## The British 'Summer'

Snow is falling through the air,
Freezing into frost on the window-pane,
The bright lights glisten on the trees,
As the snow falls like blankets.

I hear the sounds of happy children laughing,
How long till they're here and how long will they stay?
A snowball falls on the ground at my feet,
And the cold wind blows right through me.

***Deirdre Finnegan (13)***
***The Mary Erskine School***

## To Be A Witch

.

...

........

.............

Witches are nice
or are they nasty?
Full of excitement
that may end ghastly
Stirring the froth, casting their spells
Sometimes the result is just awful smells
Eye of newt and wing of bat
All done with the help of the faithful black cat
When the sun goes down, out comes the broom
Is it for fun or doom and gloom?
Fairytales tell of their wish to kill
Surely for most it's unlikely they will
So many spells are just for fun
But others could be compared to a gun
Happy and gay or cunning and sly?
A witch has no problem in making you cry
Should we be jealous or should we be sad?
The problem is likely to make us all mad
Perhaps that is the case, we are no longer sane
It's like wanting to stand in the pouring rain
I'd like to be a witch to do all the tricks
And be able to fly around on broomsticks
But what if they really are very bad?
I think I'll stay as I am, phew I'm glad.

*Jenna Owen (13)*
*The Mary Erskine School*

## My Dog

A bouncy dog,
A cuddly dog,
A chasing-after-Frisbee dog.
A spotty dog,
A dotty dog,
A swimming-in-the-river dog.
A barking dog,
A woofing dog,
A chasing-after-pigeons dog.
A hairy dog,
A shaggy dog,
A begging-for-a-biscuit dog.
A huge dog,
A lively dog,
A welcoming-me-from-school dog.
A playful dog,
A faithful dog,
In my dreams he's my dog!

***Louise McKillop (12)***
***The Mary Erskine School***

## A Witch's Cauldron

Pumpkins, goblins, witches and bats, frogs, toads, snails and cats.
This is what goes into a witch's pot.
Whether the spell works or not.
So don't mess with her or you've had your lot.
Old witches are powerful.
Young ones are bright.
So don't mess with a witch or you might just get a fright.

***Sarah Prescott (12)***
***The Mary Erskine School***

## Sunsets

Sunsets are more captivating than anything
in this entire universe.
In the coming dusk,
they are majestically seated on the Earth
in a ray of pink and orange.

They leave us slowly
with their cloak of colours,
and disappear behind a hill
on the seemingly endless horizon.

I love the way that the colours blend,
like a child's painting,
that explode like fireworks in the night sky,
that are stunning like a diamond ring.

Above all, I love them because,
they are mysterious and different
with their beautiful and golden silk touch.

***Catherine Paterson (13)***
***The Mary Erskine School***

## Bananas

Bananas taste more delicious than anything ever.
In summer they are ripe and green, in a bunch.
They peel with ease and pleasure.
I love bananas that attract me with their bright yellow colour, like the sun which helps them grow, that shines like your eyes when you take the first bite.
Above all, I love them because they are soft, succulent and taste great in a toastie with the flavours melting in your mouth.

***Chloë Johnson (13)***
***The Mary Erskine School***

## THE SPIDER

The spider sits and waits.
Patiently he watches his web.
A look of malevolence spreads across his face
A fly struggles!
Helplessly he tries to wriggle free,
from the sticky prison.
The spider emerges from his dark hole,
A dribble of saliva rolls from his greedy jaws.
He approaches the way a psychopath would his
victim!

A piercing scream suddenly echoes around the
room.
Father is summoned, and a shoe is acquired!
The spider freezes in his steps.
The stupid fly keeps on wrestling with the web.

Father merges from the hall.
A look of malevolence spreads across his face;
The slipper is tightly clasped in his hand!
A shadow slowly envelopes the spider,
And in one blow, he has met his death!

***Jenna Benson (13)***
***The Mary Erskine School***

## THE GINGER CAT

It would come right at night, on its sleek little legs,
It would pull at the washing, and take out the pegs.
It would claw at the brambles, and chase all the birds,
It would wake all the neighbours, and hear angry words.
It would eat all the plants and crawl quickly away,
Into my garden, where it would stay.

***Catherine Dods (11)***
***The Mary Erskine School***

## TORTOISES

Tortoises walk more slowly
than anything else. In their tough shell they are
more impenetrable than a high security prison
they walk with pomp and grand
posterity

I love tortoises that eat
like JCB's, that retract like a
Stanley knife, that sleep like
the dead.

Above all, I love them because
they chew
like grandads
without their false
teeth.

***Caroline Adam (13)***
***The Mary Erskine School***

## SUNSETS

Sunsets are more beautiful than anything else.
In the evening sky they die a dramatic death
In a sea of red.

I love how they demand your attention,
Casting eerie shadows over everything
And a pink hue over the world.
Like the most emotional actress,
They die a slow, painful death
Before sinking below the bloodstained horizon.

***Rowena Neville (12)***
***The Mary Erskine School***

## MISS SHEEK

The teacher looked on with a suspicious stare,
she swivelled round and got up off her
fancy new chair,
She strode to the back and in a very loud voice,
told poor little Jack that he had no choice,
he had to stay after school and copy out lessons,
for he had talked too much to
sweet Jenny Chessons.

It broke poor Jack's heart when that afternoon,
His friends decided to go play on the dunes,
he said goodbye at four o'clock square,
and hurried back to class
to carry out his dare,
he had to pour a whole pot of the strongest glue,
into Miss Sheek's very best walking shoes.

Sweet little Jenny warned him, but he took no heed,
he raced back to the classroom
to carry out the deed.

When he was done he rushed out of the class,
but he bumped into
Miss Sheek and, alas,
she started to scream, yell and curse,
at poor little Jack who just stood with her purse.

He wasn't at school for a couple of weeks,
as he was writing out lines,
for his teacher, Miss Sheek.

***Suzanne Lello (12)***
***The Mary Erskine School***

## IT'S A CAT'S LIFE

They sleep all day,
On the sofa is where they like to stay.
But when night falls,
They have to answer nature's calls.
In the morning the cats are back,
And they miaow because it's food they lack.
Then they go out to the back garden,
No matter how hard you try to guard them.
They stay out all day,
If they could talk, they'd have a lot to say.
They are good loving pets,
And love, every one of them gets.

At night they climb trees,
And scratch because they have fleas.
They eat and chase mice,
But altogether are nice.
Cats drink milk,
Some even have collars made of silk.
In the evening they curl up on the rug,
While their owners drink tea from a mug.
Cats pretend to sleep,
But when no one's looking, outside they creep.
I know that this all sounds strange,
But everything has to be in a cat's brain-range!

***Laura Amiah (12)***
***The Mary Erskine School***

## ROSE

A rose in winter is more delicate and beautiful,
than the finest feather.
In winter it stands solitary,
frozen to the ground.
Suddenly a gust of wind,
sweeps its tall thin stem into a droop.

As its blood-red petals, sway in the breeze,
the weakest of them,
float away with ease.
Stillness sets in,
and no sound is heard,
not even a chirp from a faraway bird.

Like daggers on a lifeless limb,
it pierces the skin of nature.
Slowly its petals drop off one by one,
its short life comes to an end.
And like its friends, in a few more months,
Its soul will be born again.

***Joanna Kane (13)***
***The Mary Erskine School***

## STARS!

Stars are more magical
than anything possible. In the day they are
silent watchers
in a trance of beauty. They shine
with a flow of magnificence and watch
the world from above.

I love stars that shine solitary
like an outsider, that are specks of insignificance
in the moonlit sky, that glow peacefully
like children's night-lights.

Above all, I love them because
they never fail
to leave the word in wonder
with their mysterious glow of innocence.

***Catriona Nisbet (13)***
***The Mary Erskine School***

## HALLOWE'EN

Kids run up and down the street by night,
Shouting those fatal words, 'Trick or treat, Trick or Treat,'
But how are we meant to know,
If it is a child or not, I always wonder what's under,
Their brilliant disguises, if a child or thing is hiding,
A big black bat with yellow eyes,
A small witch with broom and hat,
A cat with teeth as white as snow, or the devil in disguise,

When we go up and down the street by night,
Shouting those fatal words,
'Trick or Treat, Trick or Treat,'
I wonder to myself and think,
Is Mrs Green down the road,
Just a nice old woman, or does she chase those little girls,
And have them for her tea? Or does the man up the road,
Mr Jenkins, I think he's called,
Fly off at midnight and suck poor people's blood?
Who are these people? Are they our friends?

***Anna Hammond (12***
***The Mary Erskine School***

## Tuesday The Winner

Pleated tails with ribbons galore,
A chestnut mare gallops round the track.
Eyes big and bright, shining happily,
Excitement growing for the competition is about to begin.

And they're off, Tuesday jumps ahead,
Here comes a jump, can she clear it?
Go on girl you can do it . . .
Oh hooray! Well done!

Round the track they go,
She has such a lovely stride.
Nearing the end of the race, she looks set to win . . .
Oh good girl what a win!

Rosettes for a winner,
A cup for a winner.
What a stunning horse,
Tuesday the winner.

***Sophie Nettleton (12)***
***The Mary Erskine School***

## A Donkey

Blacky is a donkey,
the one with long ears,
he's purple and brown,
and never rears.

His house is a field,
in the countryside,
where he is as free as a bird,
and roams far and wide.

His favourite food is carrots,
he eats them all day long,
but if you thought his favourite food was grass,
you were wrong!

***Jane Cackette (11)***
***The Mary Erskine School***

## Seaside Without Sun

Water crashed against the rocks,
The beach was deserted,
Only a few dogs' footprints
Gave an indication some form of life
Had been here before.
The sky turned deep grey
Angry clouds gather threatening something
The dull sand makes a crunchy type of sound beneath my feet
An ice-cold wind dances round my face tingling my nose and ears.
Water now reaches where I stand.
This was once a jolly place.
Yet now
I pause . . . I think
How lonely, how empty!
Where are the children?
With their splendid sand castles
Where are the mothers?
With their well-prepared picnics
Where are the fathers?
With their feet buried in the sand.
The sky darkens and crisp white snowflakes begin to fall
as they hit the water they dissolve
And as I turn away
The picture I see dissolves with it!

***Tanya Valente (12)***
***The Mary Erskine School***

## Scribbles

It follows the leader,
Darting round the paper,
Round and round and round.
An I an N a K . . .
Then nothing!
A quick refill then we're off again.

This time it's doing circles,
Lots of circles, one inside the other.
On the corner of the page.
Scribbles, wiggles, fine lines, thick line, doodles.
Round and round not on the paper.
But in the washing machine . . .

My new school shirt is no longer crisp white,
But splodgey blue.
Who could have done this?
No one comes to mind but . . .
*Ink!*

***Lorna Crawford (12)***
***The Mary Erskine School***

## Hamster

Hamsters,
Look all soft and cuddly,
Children like holding them,
But when they bite,
And you feel them sink their teeth in,
And the skin broken,
And they go running to their mummies,
Though the hamster thinks,
Yum-yum what a nice piece of child.

***Katherine Hogan (11)***
***The Mary Erskine School***

## RAIN

What shape is rain?
Is it an oval, circle or square
Who knows and who cares.

I hear the rain drip from the broken pipe at night,
I hear it drip from the window-pane,
I hear it thundering down on the balcony.

Sometimes it's just spitting,
Other times it's lashing down
But when it comes, we all have fun.

There are lots of puddles outside,
Wouldn't it be fun to splash about
Let's put on our wellies and muck about.

The rain's coming down too hard to go out
But we can still have fun inside,
So we'll make a mug of cocoa and watch the rain from inside.

We're in the car driving to McDonald's
The windscreen wipers are going at full blast
It's good to be inside at McDonald's, instead of out in the rain.

The rain is so much fun
For girls and boys who are very young
So now's the time to put your coats on and come and have a bundle of fun.

***Caroline Young (11)***
***The Mary Erskine School***

## WINTER WONDERLAND

A whisper of wind, a mask of snow,
The creamy sky stood still.
A muffled breeze, the wintry trees,
The freeze was bleak and hushed.
Frozen lakes, an echo of skates,
A child's loud giggle sounded.
Rosy cheeks, bright, sharp eyes,
A mass of golden curls.
The sky went black, the girl back,
The snow began to fall.
A small white flake, a forest of trees,
A flock of birds flew south.
The world was white, a beautiful sight,
The small child gazed in wonder.

***Louise Sharp (14)***
***The Mary Erskine School***

## CHARLIE

Charlie,
What a plain name, but oh!
How it suits your fame,
How you stand in your glory,
Shining through that golden story,
You're a ray of sun in a storm,
How did I know,
My dreams would be torn?
The pace at which you run,
Makes you glint against the sun,
The gentle pound upon the ground,
Now I know what I have found.

***Sarah Dow (14)***
***The Mary Erskine School***

## Egyptian Sunset

Pyramids, black shadows
Against the flaming sky
Housed kings, their treasures
History,
The silent, silhouetted, Sphinx
Shows no emotion,
Neither wars nor triumphs will ever
Move it.

Tall graceless camels
Their oriental riders in foreign dress,
Ride by,
Kicking clouds of dust,
Oblivious to the beauty of the sunset.
Anxious to be home before
Darkness falls.

Silence reigns
Egypt invisible behind
A black cloak of darkness.
Pyramids, Sphinx, camels
Illuminated for a minute
Then gone,
As if they had never existed in an
Egyptian sunset.

***Morag MacKenzie (13)***
***The Mary Erskine School***

## SNOWBALL

The snow covered the ground with a carpet of white,
The icicles danced in the breeze,
The crispy snow was feathery and light,
Everything was still.

The sun shone brightly on that crisp December morn,
The snow sparkled in its rays,
The birds in the trees sang happily, their song,
Despite the winter days.

Among the bushes, a snowball lay,
A perfect ball of white,
Maybe a leftover from the previous day,
Or just a figure of light.

From this snowball a movement came,
Though hard to see for the sun,
Four stumpy legs and a twitching nose,
A bunny - all in one!

He stretched out his limbs and gave a big yawn,
His nose still twitching away,
With his pure-white fur as soft as the snow,
No animal looked sweeter than he did that day.

***Fiona Steedman (13)***
***The Mary Erskine School***

## Life In Spring

I wake up to see the sun shining in my window,
and feel the warm sun heating me up.

I hear the cheerful sounds of the sweet birds,
flying around in the sky above.

The newborn lambs are out this lovely morning,
to learn to walk and do the things their mothers do.

The beautiful daffodils growing to their heights,
all trying to reach the sun.

I wonder how all these nice things happen.
Is it to please my eager eyes
or is it just there for pleasure?

In the dark of the night they will grow by secret sight.
They will grow tall and strong but only with the gifts
from us.

As I walk in the garden I hear the happy sounds of all
God's creatures.

I hear and see these wonderful things all around me in
this exciting world.

***Natalie McNaught (12)***
***The Mary Erskine School***

## ALONE

The old man hobbled along,
He found his place on the stone cold pavement,
This is where he would sleep tonight,
Just like the last and the night before that.

The crisp white snow lay around him,
Still, sad and lonely.
He sat and watched,
Thinking about his future,
And his past.

His memories, clear and vivid,
Never fading, always there,
His blanket, his protection,
His face, his mask,
Disguising the bygone times.

Till his eyes were tired,
He gently closed them,
And he remembered no more,
For a while.

***Paula Yau (14)***
***The Mary Erskine School***

## THE ENVIRONMENT

Our environment is dying
And we are the culprits
Polluting the atmosphere every day
Where are our merits?

Many species; tiger, panda and gorilla
Are becoming extinct every day
And we just continue on with our little busy lives
Unaware of our terrible fray.

If we all just stop and think,
Maybe just for a moment
About the way we live our lives
We could save the environment!

***Emily Shaw (14)***
***The Mary Erskine School***

## THAT WINDOW

I can see many things out of that window,
Trees,
Houses,
Cars,
Telephone wires,
But the thing I see most is the sky.
Out of all those things I see out of that window,
Trees,
Houses,
Cars,
Telephone wires,
And the sky,
The one I like best is the sky.
Why?
Because it changes colour
From blue to
Pink,
Purple,
Black,
Orange and
Yellow.
So when I look out of that window,
I see the most colourful thing,
The sky.

***Athene Kate Greig (14)***
***The Mary Erskine School***

## Dr Z's Decision

Who lives?
Mr X
Or Mr Y.
Do I kill Mr X
To try to save Mr Y,
Or should I let Mr Y die
Then Mr X might too.
Whoever lives
Whoever dies,
It's up to me.
Their lives in my hands.
One switch,
One life.
One might live,
Both might not.
Few people will know
In the years to come,
But I'll know who lived,
And who did not.
Mr X
Or Mr Y.

***Catherine Alice Crowe (14)***
***The Mary Erskine School***

## Control

Walls closing within the mind,
Getting smaller by the second,
The burning of the incessant brain
Lost control of those things around

Love, fear, hate and hurt
All fill the space only inches wide,
Names once not questioned, whirl in the never ending waves
Of thoughts which crash mindlessly about

The strange, old surroundings,
Lose the way forward
Only to go back on the emotional, real
Losing of the present self control

Reality is lost in the bubbling broth
As years are centuries
And time never turns nor waits
As I sit and wait.

***Lily A Humphries (13)***
***The Mary Erskine School***

## A WINTER'S TALE

A sprinkling of sugar, spreads like sand.
Gusting wind sweeps across the land,
Dancing, swirling, playing games,
Whispering as if singing names.

Children laughing, having fun
Snowballs flying through the air.
The sun now sets to dusky purple
Night now lives, a moon so fair.

All is alive, the shadows jigging
Climbing up the yacht's rigging,
Cooing of the owl's dull tone
All night long the same old drone.

A peep of light now fills the sky,
The morning call from a neighbouring horse,
Sparrows chirping whilst they aimlessly fly,
A winter's tale now takes its course.

***Rebecca Erdal (14)***
***The Mary Erskine School***

## THE WRITER

He sat staring at the empty page pondering,
At which words he should choose to write.
He sat and waited, trying to paint a picture with words
But it seemed as though his paintbrush was bone dry.

Ideas were running a marathon inside his mind,
But nothing seemed attractive at all, just a jumble of images
Together, not wanting to transform themselves,
Into something wonderful for everyone to enjoy.

For sentences there needed to be many words,
Hundreds of letters which would make a scene,
A performance would be put on as the page came to life
Colourful, witty and exciting just as writing should be.

The minutes were feeling more like hours as he tried,
Tried so hard to let the thoughts flow through his mind.
The writer's mind was filled with many different pictures
But it seemed like there was nothing that was enticing him.

Suddenly, like a bolt of lightning, a thought shot into his head,
If he had no inspiring thoughts, then why not write about *that?*
So the writer sat and hurriedly wrote about what had encouraged him,
It seemed as though the gallery had its painting after all.

***Suzanne Boobis (13)***
***The Mary Erskine School***

## The Show

The preparation; the waiting,
Rehearsals and lines,
Blood, sweat and tears,
Hours, days and weeks.

Nearing the time, closer now,
The stress, mounting and mounting,
The stage, lights and make-up,
Closer and closer all the time.

The night has arrived,
All is ready, and prepared,
Only awaiting for something,
Anything, to go wrong.

***Fiona Ross (13)***
***The Mary Erskine School***

## Autumn Leaves

A rich array of colours: brown, gold, red and yellow.
Twisting, turning, twirling.
Spinning 360°, before dancing to the ground.
Flitting, floating, fluttering -
Delicately like butterflies.
Swirling, scrunching, crunching, crackling, crisp.
A colourful carpet of rustling autumn leaves, lying on the ground.

***Claire Alexander (13)***
***The Mary Erskine School***

## THE SPIRITS OF PEACE

As we walk the war torn corridors of the hospital,
which wind like the walls of memory we once had,
the blank and weary faces of the staff twist into,
one expression, worn by those who have seen too
much suffering,
Although the sense of sterility haunts every corner,
the ruined building is contaminated by our presence.
We see the flashes of life of the exhausted patients
who have escaped our limitless grasp but some day,
they will join us.
Many messages of grief are sent to loved ones who
grieve for those we have taken, whose pain we have stopped
and injuries we healed as only we could.
We were once like them, we felt the loss of our companions
their precious lives taken by the ravages of war,
so like the many others that have been and shall come,
until we joined them and became what we are now,
A friend to the sick, the relievers of all pain which
cannot be cured.
We cut through the final strands of life, as we take them
to the light at the end of the darkest tunnels, to
the heaven they made for themselves on earth
as we hope that the fighting will end and that the lives
of so many innocents will never be taken again.

***Nadin Hadi (14)***
***The Mary Erskine School***

## Storms In Spring

It started with a cloud; dark and distant.
A single drop of rain
Fell,
An omen
Of the commencing storm.
A dense black cape covered the golden sky,
Smothering, stunning.

Birds flew back to their nests
In a rush of wings and song -
Echoing in the memory seconds after a new note had begun.
Circles of rain exploded onto the river,
Fallen like their fathers and forefathers.
Old forgotten glasses and cups filled with rain,
The bicycle at the bottom of the garden rusting.

It stopped raining and the sun appeared,
Having fought and won the battle of the skies.
Several ribbons of merged colour then came forth
Bold and bright,
Triumphant in their form.
They lay in a curve - one on top of the other
In the most simple but beautiful of phenomena.

I stood immersed in this loveliness,
Blinked,
And it was gone.
The blackbirds sang in protest,
The leaves rustled in sorrow,
The winds went into retreat
And the storm passed.

***Caitlin Smith (17)***
***Trinity Academy***

## World Of Words

The words we use in life,
Can be happy, can be sad,
The words we use in life,
Can be good, can be bad.

Soft, sweet, sugary words,
Float around the sky.
Upon pure white silky clouds,
They dance and they lie.

Big insulting black words
Blast inside your heart.
These awful words
Can tear you apart.

In your imagination
Words float through your brain.
In dark woods, damp passages
And very spooky lanes.

Bricks can build lots of things,
But words can build more.
Words can build imagination,
Words can build heaven's door.

Words can be stupid,
Words can be clever.
You should use them now,
It is better than never.

Words are what we use,
Every day in the world.
There are lots of words,
Out there to be found and unfurled.

***Kathryn Whitelaw (12)***
***Trinity Academy***

## I AM

I am good
I am happy
I am an angel

I am bad
I am sad
I'm the devil

What am I?

I feel joy
I am normal
I am healthy

I feel pain
I'm insane
I am sick

What am I?

I am young
I am asked
I understand

I am old
I am told
I'm confused

What am I?

The answer is plain to see
What am I?
I am *me!*

***Megan Francis (12)***
***Trinity Academy***

## A FIELD OF HORSES

Kept together with a fence all round,
Dug deep down in the cold hard ground.
They want to be free to do what they like,
But they've been imprisoned by a guy called Mike.
He brings them food, water and hay,
But they want to go far away.
Every day they want to leave,
But they can't, what would it achieve?
They would be caught and brought right back,
Then food, water and hay they would lack.

***Danielle Thomson (13)***
***Trinity Academy***

## World

The world is made up of so many places,
So many people and so many faces.
I look into a mirror and see myself,
But not my inside,
Not deep inside my soul.
When you see someone,
Don't just see their colour,
Not their face.
Look deep inside their soul.
We are all in the same world,
The same place,
It's not going to change.
People are not colours,
Faces,
Places,
People are hearts,
Souls,
Minds,
People are people.

***Caroline Spencer (12)***
***Trinity Academy***

## School

School is where all children go,
To learn about subjects they will need to know,
From 8.30 to 3.30 we try our best,
Learning maths, English and all the rest.

My favourite subject is PE,
Lots of games and exercise suits me,
Hockey and basketball I like to play,
I would love to play them every day.

Teachers range from good to bad,
Some are happy but some are sad,
They give us homework to do at night,
And I always hope I get it right.

I hope to do well at Trinity,
To go on to uni,
And get a degree,
So I will need to work hard and try my best,
And study hard for every test.

***Claire Day (13)***
***Trinity Academy***

## THE DEATH OF MY BELOVED PET, HONEY

As I watch the unconscious creature on my lap,
I realise that I would never have the pleasure
Of the ginger creature running around the house,
Never again touch her soft coat,
Never see her gorgeous face greet me as I return
Never to see her again,
And yet I wonder why,
Why a creature of such splendour should leave
This world.
This world of hatred,
Now I look at the peaceful body in the box,
And I wonder if it was my fault,
My fault that she had died,
My fault that I would never see her run around,
My fault that I would never see her sweet face greet me
My fault that I would never see her again.

***Nadia Petriconi (12)***
***Trinity Academy***

## No Winners But Losers

The protesters marched along the street,
Chanting together in time to their feet,
Preparing themselves for what was ahead,
Wondering if someone might end up dead.

There was Peter O'Maley who worked in a garage,
Five children at home and a failing marriage.
There was Alan and Sue who were in it together,
Both faces grey, just like the weather.

Banners were risen, so too were flags,
Some carried weapons in polythene bags.
Knives and clubs, hidden away,
Carefully placed so not on display.

The men at the front were brought to a standstill,
By the screech of a whistle, piercing and shrill.
Then the enemy came into sight,
And in that second, out broke a fight.

Grant and Mitch fought two against one,
Then felt sick at what they had done.
Jamie Firt wondered 'Why?'
As his bloody fist rose to the sky.
He felt the crunch of bone on bone,
And the body below gave out a low moan.
David Mill felt the stab of a knife,
And realised that this was the end of his life.

In the dawn the next morning, not a soul to be seen,
A paper bag blown, torn at the seam.
The street resembled a battleground,
Where no winners or losers had been found.

***Sophie Simpson (13)***
***Trinity Academy***

## THE SOLDIER'S CALL

Out we marched in rows of ten,
Hundreds of us, but thousands of them.
We're in battle to fight till the end,
So I'm waving goodbye, goodbye to my friends.
I look at the men all ready to fight,
They could be dead before this new night.
I ask myself, why do we fight?
We're fighting for freedom and our country's right.
We fight to defend and not to invade,
But we need a miracle to come to our aid.
To save our country, where people run free,
To save our country, hear our plea.
I don't want to fight, I know it is wrong,
But I must help the land we've held for so long.
My urge to fight is weak, although the call of the others is strong,
I must follow my line of duty, although I feel it is wrong.
I look at the men who want to run free,
I plead to the enemy, please let me be.
But what's freedom if you're not alive?
To be a hero, you have to survive.

***Chloe Shoniwa (12)***
***Trinity Academy***

## COMPUTERS

Computers,
We create them,
We upgrade them,
We create artificial intelligence,
They rule us!

***Euan McDougall (12)***
***Trinity Academy***

## WORLDLY ATOMS

Question. How was the world created?
Do we really care however?
If you consider all the possibilities about the world's creation.
For which is needed keen observation,
Like mine,
You would know that none of the theories are actually true to life.
Except mine, created in severe strife.

Forget the big bang,
Which to some scientists started the universe developing from a haze,
Or even the existence of God,
Who created the world inside seven days,
Who would believe this,
Not me!
I couldn't even build a Lego toy within a week.

The true story is all to do with atoms.
If you consider the fact that our world,
Or even our entire universe
Was in fact a universe within universes within one tiny atom,
An atom underneath the fingernail of someone
Anyone in another place,
And that the same is happening to them under another person's fingernail,
Or even under a toenail.

Even we could have billions of dimensions and worlds within us.
Hiroshima in my view wasn't a nuclear bomb,
All it was is the person's fingernail that we are under got cracked over Japan,
Hence major death and destruction.
The way the world is!

***David Pickavance (17)***
***Trinity Academy***

## Forest Song

The velvet purple sky hangs low over the land;
And the moon shines through the mist like a diamond,
Casting a shadow on the trees.
The call of the eagle echoes through the sky,
As he soars across the lake.
The wind whispers a delicate tune;
And the wolf howls a lonely cry at the moon.
The leaves on the trees rustle quietly.
Then all is still,
And the forest sleeps.

***Kirsty Macqueen (11)***
***Trinity Academy***

## Chocolate

Once the chocolate has entered your mouth . . .

You have stepped inside,
The ultimate chocolate ride.

You feel the chocolate melt in your mouth . . .

The liquid goes down your chest,
Where it's all warm and at its best.

But all too soon it's over . . .

Then your teacher pulls you out from maths,
And says, 'You've got detention for eating in class!'

***Clare Milligan (13)***
***Trinity Academy***

## BOSNIA

A place of disease, a place of hurt,
A thriving community now in the dirt.
The injured are bleeding,
A child is pleading, 'All my family are dead,
Please put a roof over my head.'

A soldier's shout, a girl screams out,
A bomb is dropped, a pistol is popped.
Among all the blood, guts and gore,
It's obvious now what's come is war.

Although the fighting is no more,
Some are still homeless and some are still sore.
So spare a thought or a penny or two,
And thank the Lord it wasn't you.

***Emma Timons (12)***
***Trinity Academy***

## NOTHING

'Nothing' is what you were doing last night,
'Nothing' is what you're hiding behind your back.
'Nothing' is what you were talking about
for an hour on the phone.
'Nothing' is what you were day-dreaming
about all morning.
'Nothing' is what was written on that
piece of paper you just passed to your friend.

'Nothing' is what's in your stomach before
breakfast.

'Nothing' is just . . . 'Nothing'!

***Judy Miller (11)***
***Trinity Academy***

## I Run In Fear

I run in fear,
Whenever he is near,
He's scared away all my friends,
The torture never ends.

I am but a worm,
Below him I struggle and squirm,
Nobody stands up for me,
For they are all afraid of he.

My size, my clothes, my accent and my family,
He doesn't realise just how miserable my life can be,
My confidence has faded away,
He taunts, laughs and sneers at me,
Every day.

So next time you are just about,
To yell at someone,
Kick or shout,
Please think about how you would feel,
Should you be put through this ordeal.

***Catherine Miller (13)***
***Trinity Academy***

## Bed

By a hospital bed
Not so long ago
I sat.
In the bed
Lay a man
Asleep, far away.
He dreamt the day and night away,
What was he dreaming?
I asked myself
Or was he half dead?
I did not know . . .

Along came the day
He gave me a smile
And then I knew
That he's going to stay with me
For a very long while.

***Arwen Buchanan (12)***
***Trinity Academy***